WINES, VINES AND THINGS

Wines, Vines and

Things

by

W. Scott Richards

WINES, VINES AND THINGS

Published by Loch Haven Enterprises, LLC
P.O. Box 33, Milford, VA 22514

First Edition

ISBN 9781 499327502

WINES, VINES AND THINGS

Table of Contents

THINGS CONTINUED - REVIEWS

ACKNOWLEDGEMENTS

I thank God for the talent He has given me. In His wisdom it lay dormant for years, but was brought out in His time.

I would be remiss not to thank my wife, Diane, who patiently and thoroughly edited this work. Her work of love on this book is beyond value to me. She not only taught me how to hit a softball, she showed me a lot about writing and encouraged me in this venture.

Toni Stinson, as editor of the Caroline Progress gave me my first break, with the column From the Vine. I owe a lot to all the editors I have worked with at the Caroline Progress.

When From the Vine stopped running, Rob and Virginia Grogan of the Fredericksburg Front Porch picked me up. I had no where else to turn, and though it was not a paid column, it gave me lots of experience and exposure. I continue to write for them to this day.

To the many who have read my work and have given me feedback, I am forever grateful.

I am thankful for my third grade teacher, Margaret Pease, who made me write sentences in class and commented on my report card at the end of the year, "…someday Scott may be an author." A vision that has stayed with me ever since.

INTRODUCTION

I have always read. I mean really read, a lot. As I have grown, so has my fascination with words and the pictures they paint in my mind. Interestingly enough, I never liked to write. I attribute that to the fact that my fine motor skills were not the best, so putting a pen to paper was a difficult thing to do (please understand I reference the age prior to computers).

In the second grade, I became captivated with the books the teacher kept in the classroom, taking a pile of them home and returning them the next day; all of them read. My parents bought my older brother tons of books when he was young, but he never read them. That's right, I did. One of my best Christmas gifts when I was young was the complete set of A. A. Milne's *Winnie the Pooh.* It was a treasure to me. I remember being in my room on a Sunday afternoon reading a book about the Alamo. I had just finished the book when my mother started giving me the riot act about spending too much time inside. Being a compliant child, I went outside to play, only to find my mind still in the book, making everything around me seem so very strange.

I can remember as a pre-teen reading the editorial page and arguing with my parents about the points the editors were trying to make. My father tried reading me the Sunday comics to divert me but it did not work.

In middle school, my pastor baited and hooked me, giving me first J.R.R. Tolkien's *The Hobbit.* I devoured it and begged for more, going through the entire *Lord of the Rings* Trilogy.
It was then my pastor not only set the hook, but he set my mind on fire, giving me a box filled with science fiction. The works of Ray Bradbury, Isaac Asimov, and Robert Heinlein to name a few became my diet, ever expanding an already overactive imagination.

High school brought such authors Upton Sinclair, Chaim Potok, and Chaucer to my venue. One of the best retreats I had during my teen years was in a book. As an adult, I have added authors and deleted them, sampled some and read the entire works of others. Still to this day, the list grows.

I began college studying math because I thought I would not have to write lengthy term papers. After flunking out of the math department in my junior year, I changed my major to philosophy and religion as a pre ministerial study. Although I found the subject matter interesting, I hated the idea of putting any work at all in a paper and turned in many fresh off the typewriter with little or no editing done.

As an adult, I began to study wine. My years of the study of wine for the longest time resulted in my years of the study of wine and not much else. In April 2008, I began taking medication for adult ADD. Two weeks into the medication, I wrote a short column about wine events in Virginia and submitted it to a the Caroline Progress, which is the weekly paper in Caroline County. The editor called me and said she wanted to speak with me about doing a weekly column. I remember walking out of our house with a bottle of 2005 Bordeaux and two wine glasses to meet with the editor, when my wife, Diane, arrived home from work. I do not remember what I said to her, but I was off to begin my career as a writer. On that day I was fifty three years old and about to be published for the first time.

I started writing about wine, because that is what I professed to know something about. In 2011, Diane and I planted Loch Haven Vineyards in Sparta, Virginia and my association with growers in Virginia has given me a lot to write about. The scope of my writing expanded into the local community, in particular, sports and events at the area high school. Covering Caroline High School has provided not only stories, but also has given me the privilege of watching young athletes develop both academically and athletically.

I would have to say that life itself has been the deepest well I had to draw for my writing. It has not been always fun. Situations in my life were not supposed to happen as they did, I had a much smoother plan in mind. Through it all, God had a much more decisive purpose for my life than I imagined. It makes me glad that He is God, and I am just a man.

This book, a collection of writings I have accumulated over the past years, is about wine, because wine was my initial study; vines, because it is in the vineyard that wine is made; and the things life is made of, which is why I drink wine. It is also a discovery of a God given gift that laid dormant for decades. The development of my writing skills over the years has proven to be a great source of encouragement, causing me to marvel at what has been revealed, and giving ground to an excitement for what lies ahead.

Winos, Vines and Things.
Enjoy.

Without question, the greatest invention in the history of mankind is wine. Oh, I grant you that the wheel was also a fine invention, but the wheel does not go nearly as well with pizza.

-Dave Berry

WINES

IT STARTED WITH A CHOCOLATE CHIP COOKIE
January, 2012

It did not actually start there, but the chocolate chip cookie is an excellent point in which to begin.

My mother's side of our family was rather large with four girls and one boy and they all remained close. The main gathering point for the family was always at Grandma and Papa Lynn's house. It was not unusual to walk into their house and be greeted by thirty or forty people who included aunts, uncles, great aunts, cousins, grandparents from spouses of the original five and an entire pack of dogs (no one from out-of-town had the heart to leave their dogs at home and miss all the festivities).

The table was laden with food that served as a grazing area as people came and went from all parts of the Commonwealth of Virginia. The real treasure chest for the grandchildren was the refrigerator. There seemed to be an endless supply of sodas of which Grandma distributed very liberally, much to the chagrin of our parents.

There was a lot of people who drank heavily amongst our family. As a result of this extra curricular activity, there was a lot of drinking paraphernalia to be had by anyone concerned. It seemed to interest my cousin Frances Ann and myself more than others in that we loved to drink our sodas out of a shot glass emulating the cowboys at bars in westerns we saw on television.

I must interject at this point a rule of the Lynn household. Children were allowed to sip from their parents drinks until the age of four or five and then were cut off until they reached drinking age. Of course, when the entire family got together, there was always an older cousin who managed to get some liquor or beer and was always more than happy to show off by allowing the younger cousins to taste. Often as not, there was also that occasional drink that was laid down and forgotten by an adult which came to the attention of the cousins and was passed around with great abandon.

On very seldom seen occasions, we would be allowed to have a small glass of wine if there were not that many people around. I remember sitting on Grandma Lynn's couch sipping white wine and eating one of the ever present chocolate chip cookies from the kitchen and thinking what an excellent pairing that made. I am, to this day, somewhat partial to chocolate chip cookies with a good sauvignon blanc.

Since that time, I have watched cousins and aunts and uncles go through various phases of drinking with all but a few being able to control the urges to imbibe too much. Throughout all of that, my mind still goes back to the cheap white or red wine that was drunk. Maybe it is a psychological thing, but today, wine remains my go to drink. And to think it all started with a chocolate chip cookie.

BACCHUS AND WINE
August, 2014

With all the DNA talk going around, whether one watches the crime shows on television or not, hearing about DNA being used to keep track of wine varietals developed is not surprising. The Sangiovese vines in my own vineyard can be traced to Italy.

Some think of Italy as where wine originated. Of course, the French say they are not only the origin, but the center of the wine world as well. Unfortunately, DNA verifies neither. What is left to answer this all important question is tradition. One tradition states wine comes from yet another location, Sicily.

As the story goes, Bacchus was sent down from Mount Olympus to introduce wine to mortals on the island of Sicily. Descending from the Mountain of the Gods, he carried in his hand a grape vine planted in the hollow of the bone of a bird. The vine grew as he travelled towards Sicily. Halfway on his journey, the vine was transplanted to the hollow of a bone of a lion. By the time the destination was reached, the vine had grown so much it was moved to the hollow of the bone of a mule.

Bacchus landed at Sicily, planted, nurtured and developed the vine, taking shoots and starting other vines until he ended up with a large vineyard. From the fruit of the vineyard, he made wine, thus providing for mankind their first taste. So the story goes.

This tradition, as with many good stories, contains a moral, which of course is about wine. One drinks a little wine and may be flighty as a bird. Given some more, they become courageous as a lion. However, when too much wine is consumed, one tends to have the demeanor of a jack ass.

There are no definitive answers as to the origins of wine, but one thing remains, wine is a drink to be taken responsibly.

CHOCO WINE
March, 2015

Even after Valentine's Day with all its gooey chocolaty confections has passed, the thought of chocolate still remains. To be honest, it has always been there. Valentine's Day means nothing to the luscious, dark brown, delectable treat (with or without nuts), because chocolate does not take a holiday, tempting people 24 hours a day, seven days a week. A big deal is made about some stores not having candy at the check out line so children will not be tempted to eat something we adults say they do not really need. What about the adults? Who says that we are so temptation proof we can just saunter by the Snicker's Bars and not be affected? Okay, end of confession, time to move on.

Wine used to be the area where anyone tempted by chocolate would be safe. Granted, there are some very good wines for those with a sweet tooth. But generally speaking there was not much overlay between wine and chocolate. However, in recent years, the gauntlet has been dropped and the challenge faces chocoholics squarely. Chocolate wine, there ought-a be a law. Maybe it is because I am trying to show how tough I am, but I usually keep a bottle of chocolate wine on hand, untouched mind you.

My first taste of chocolate wine was not a pleasant one. Please bear with me, this is my opinion, and it has evolved through much research and taste testing. There are two types of this concoction, as alike as good and evil. First, let us look at the evil one. Think back to the best milkshake you have ever had. It was made with real ice cream and whole milk, or even better yet, cream and then mixed up in one of those thingies in the ice cream parlor in a metal cup. The taste was rich and chocolaty, so thick your straw collapses. After the shake was poured into the cup, the waitress set the metal cup down beside you with the

5

remainder of the shake that did not fit into the cup.

Now imagine this bit of chocolate Americana made with a creamy, Dutch chocolate blend. Yummy. Then all of a sudden, there is this taste that has nothing to do with the chocolate flavor and actually causes your taste buds to curdle. What is it? Wine, of course! You have just tasted the failure of a wine blend. Just because it is alcohol, does not mean wine goes well with everything. A popular form of chocolate wine is a wonderful chocolate drink infused with wine. Two good things put together in a totally incorrect manner.

Back to the drawing board. But wait, Cooper Vineyards in Virginia has already taken that step. Dismantling the aforesaid tragedy, the winemakers at Coopers have put it back together in a most pleasing way, to be referred to as the good, or right one in deference to the evil one previously described. In this case, instead of starting with chocolate, wine is the base. Norton wine, made from a native Virginia grape, developed by Dr. Norton on Belle Isle in Richmond and popular until prohibition, has again become a popular wine in the Old Dominion and is the wine of choice for this chocolate delight. Infused into the wine is chocolate, giving this dark wine a brown tint. Even the nose is chocolate. The real test comes with the taste, which is more like a deep, dark cocoa blended in perfectly with the musky taste of the Norton wine.

You have just experienced *Noche,* Cooper Vineyards' contribution to this realm of wine that few make correctly. This includes not just Virginia wines, but wines from all over the country. Virginians can stand proud. More than just being the Napa of the East, as the taste of *Noche* shows, Virginia has developed the top chocolate wine.

Drink out of your own back yard, and remember, Virginia is for wine, Napa is for auto parts.

THE NEW JUICE BOX
July, 2011

Tell most people who have been drinking wine for a while that you drink wine from a box and you probably will get a look of confusion, sympathy or disdain, or a combination of the three. Why would anyone stoop so low as to drink the swill that comes packaged in a cardboard box? At one time, I must admit, I would have been aghast at the notion of people who did not know better settling for less, when, for just a few dollars more much better wine was theirs for the asking.

One advantage of box wines is that the wine is in a bladder contained in a cardboard box in such a way that as the wine is consumed, the bladder decreases in size allowing no air to mix in with the wine causing it to go bad. Also, because the bladder is in a cardboard box, the wine is not affected by light. On average, a three liter box of wine can last up to four weeks without going bad. Combine this with the fact that the bladder and the cardboard box are much cheaper than four seven hundred fifty milliliter bottles and the answer is simple to see which is more cost effective. This brings us back to the original situation, why do serious wine drinkers look down their noses at box wines?

In times past most box wines were truly worthy of the disdain heaped upon them. The juices were the bottom of the barrel with the idea of making a quick dollar off of something most wine makers believed should have been thrown away. Black Box Wines has invested in premium juices for their boxed wines and are proving to many nay sayers, with such wines as their Black Box Cabernet Sauvignon, that box wine can be an excellent and inexpensive product for those who are looking for an everyday wine but do not feel comfortable paying an exorbitant amount. In addition, Corbett Canyon Pinot Noir was tried and found to have a very nice depth of fruit with a medium finish that would give all but the most discerning of palettes no impression that it originated in a box.

Admittedly, not all box wines meet the standard that these two wines have achieved, but they are not the only ones to have achieved this status. The best way to describe the box wine industry is, "the good, the bad and the cubic."

AND THIS IS MY BLEND…
October, 2014

The Virginia wine industry is constantly changing. As the growth of the number of wineries leads to a more competitive market, the development of the facilities and their usage becomes more apparent.

Tasting rooms are more elaborate. Gone are the bare bones rooms where wine is poured in cheap nondescript glasses. Those pouring the wine are required to be knowledgable not only about the wines they are serving, but they must also be able answer the many questions about the winery operation as well.

One humorous narrative tells of a couple who visited a winery with a tasting room in a one room cinder block shack. In the room was a board about four feet long with cinder blocks stacked under each end. On one end was a jug of red wine and on the opposite end was a jug of white wine. A rather unkempt man who looked as if he lived out among the vines stood welcoming the couple to his winery. A single glass was put on the board.

Picking up the jug of white wine, he said, "This is my white."

Next, picking up the jug of red wine he said, "This is my red."

While pouring both wines into the glass simultaneously, he declared with a loud voice, "And this is my blend!"

Wineries are being used as wedding venues. As a result, not only the tasting rooms, but the grounds have become elaborate to attract those looking for a place to hold their nuptials. While many wineries have small kitchens to accommodate caterers for receptions, more are actually employing chefs to provide meals designed to show off their wines while providing a food service as part of the wedding package.

Concerts are another activity being enjoyed at wineries. Everything from acoustical to classical music have become attractions. Concerts given on the grounds are presented either with food provided or concert goers are invited to bring a picnic lunch to enjoy with their favorite wine from the winery. At a barrel tasting I was working at a winery in central Virginia, a singer was performing with an acoustical guitar and the people watching were not only enjoying the wine offered, but many had lit cigars sold there.

At Good Luck Cellars near Kilmarnock, Virginia, some of the functions offer book signings and opera companies in their repertoire of events, raising the bar once more as to what can be found at a winery. Many I have visited have a fireplace somewhere in the tasting room. What a wonderful place for a small library. How much better does it get than to enjoy a glass of good wine while reading a book by the fireplace as a string quartet plays in the background? Don't laugh, tasting rooms are evolving at too great a pace.

Whether you drink a wine in your own home or choose to go to a tasting room, enjoy! Here's to Virginia wines, cheers!

GLUHWEIN
December, 2014

When I was growing up, every Christmas eve at our church we had a Moravian Love Feast. I am not Moravian but it was a nice service, particularly afterwards. In our fellowship hall there were always Christmas cookies served with a hot spiced tea. The taste of the tea has remained with me throughout the years. Of course, it is no longer called spiced tea, the term in the proper circles is *mulled tea*. Whatever term is used, it makes me think of Christmas.

Now that I have gotten older, I am able to expand my repertoire beyond mulled tea to include mulled wine, or as the Germans call it, *Gluhwein*. This holiday beveridge is best described as a hot toddy and is made up of red wine that has been spiced with cinnamon sticks, cloves, star aniseed, citrus and sugar, in proportions according to the taste of the consumer. My personal favorite is gluhwein mit Schuss (or shot). For the Schuss, cognac works well, giving this German drink an international feel. The mixture is heated but not boiled as boiling will cause the alcohol to dissipate, a tragedy unless one decides to have a nonalcoholic toddy. If the gluhwein is already made, three quarters of a mug microwaved for forty five seconds is just about perfect. I would recommend adding the Schuss after the gluhwein is heated.

Gluhwein, or glowing wine, is said to have been named in reference to hot irons used for mulling. Some say that the makeup of the drink is a result of individuals adding spices to wine that was going bad in order to keep from having to throw it away. Attributed to the Germans, this holiday treat is documented as far back as 1490 to a tankard of gluhwein owned by Count John IV of Katzeneinbogen, a German nobleman who is also credited with being the first to grow the Riesling grape.

Today, gluhwein is enjoyed in Germany in Christmas markets along with Lebkuchen, a spice cake from Nuremberg and renowned throughout the country. In the United States, it is good with whatever Christmas treats are nearby. Gluhwein can be bought at the most wine stores. For the adventurous, here is a recipe:

INGREDIENTS

3/4 cup orange juice or water, if preferred

3/4 cup sugar (to taste)

1 cinnamon stick

1 whole nutmeg

1 star anise pod

1 orange

10 whole cloves

1 (750 ml) bottle of red wine - a red German wine or a good hearty red wine.

DIRECTIONS

In a sauce pan, combine orange juice, sugar, cinnamon stick, nutmeg, and star anise. Bring to a boil, reduce heat and simmer.

Cut the orange in half and squeeze the juice into the simmering liquid. Push the cloves into the outside of the orange peel and place the peel in the simmering liquid. Continue simmering for 30 minutes, until the liquid has been reduced to a thick syrup.

Pour in the wine, heat until steaming but not simmering. If it simmers with the wine included, the alcohol will cook off. Remove clove-orange peels.Serve hot in mugs.

This recipe serves 6, but can be expanded to serve more. Make a day in advance and keep sealed in the refrigerator overnight. Like Sangria, the flavors will meld together.

OYSTERS AND THE OYSTER TRAIL
August, 2014

Oysters are alive and well in Virginia thanks to the efforts of companies like the Rappahannock River Oyster Company in Topping, Virginia, run by Travis and Ryan Croxton, the great grandsons of founder James Arthur Croxton, Jr. In 2014, the oyster industry celebrated the largest harvest since 1987. After just twelve years, the oyster harvest has increased from 23,000 to more than 500,000 bushels annually. In 2013 this industry brought in $22 million dollars dockside. As if made in heaven, the oyster industry in the Old Dominion has paired with another burgeoning industry, Virginia wines.

In August of 2014, Senator Mark Warner (Dem-Va) visited the Rappahannock River Oyster Company as he toured the Northern Neck promoting the oyster industry in Virginia. I stood with a group of media people trying hard not to look like one of them.

As he and a number of people went out to inspect the oyster beds in the Rappahannock River, he turned to me and said, "Scott, you're going with me in my boat, aren't you?" Not knowing what else to do, I retorted, "Of course!"

After we were in the oyster beds for a while, to my surprise, I noticed another boat approaching with its passengers laden with cameras and other such media equipment. Then it hit me, that was the media boat I was supposed to be in!

As the second boat pulled along side, Warner leaned over to them and said, "You guys are too late, Scott has an exclusive on this one!"

Warner's interest and knowledge of the Chesapeake Bay Oyster was evident as he discussed Virginia's role in bringing new life into the industry with Travis Croxton and Dr. John T. Wells, director of the Virginia Institute of Marine Science.

While in the beds, several oysters were shucked allowing Warner, along with Middlesex County Sheriff David P. Bushey, to enjoy the Bay's bounty. Once ashore, raw oysters on the half shell, courtesy of Warner, were consumed with a choice of beer or white wine.

In 1899, James Arthur Croxton, Jr. started the Rappahannock River Oysters Company on five acres of the Rappahannock River. A family tradition began and continues today. Despite discouragement against continuing in the oyster business by some members of the Croxton family, Travis and Ryan Croxton revitalized the company in 2002 and put themselves in a position to be sending oysters to every state in the country as well as Hong Kong and Thailand.

In 2005 Food & Wine Magazine awarded them the "Tastemaker's Award," given to people who changed the world of food and wine by the time they reached thirty five. Rappahannock Oysters is one of many oyster companies who are bringing more oysters to the market and developing beds which help to cleanse the waters of the Chesapeake Bay.

On August 19, 2014, Virginia Governor McAuliffe kicked off the Virginia Oyster Trail at the Governor's mansion in Richmond to connect visitors to the state with the oyster industry. Featured were oysters from the seven regions around the Chesapeake Bay paired with Virginia Wines. Governor and Ms. McAuliffe encouraged listeners Virginia oysters are something to brag about just as Maine does about their lobsters.

While many of the oysters (all raw and on the half shell) paired with Chardonnay, several oyster companies chose pinot grigio or sauvignon blanc, which provided for a refreshing accompaniment without being washed away by the brininess of the oysters.

The Virginia Oyster Trail and the many Virginia Wine Trails unite oysters and wine into a perfect pairing. Oysters, like wine, reflect their environment on one's palette. The oysters of

Rappahannock River Oysters, LLC, from the headwaters of the Rappahannock River provide a mixture of minerality and sweetness; the ones from the Eastern Shore harvested by Ruby Salts exhibited a strong briny taste. The Virginia Oyster Trail kick off provided oyster lovers the opportunity for individuals to determine for themselves the differences between harvest locations in addition to being an excellent promotion for the joining of two distinctive Virginia products.

The Virginia Oyster Trail and the Virginia Wine Trails, a pairing in taste no other state can touch.

WINE AND OYSTERS
April, 2015

Summer is officially over and people are making their final trips to the beach, or they are going to get the cheaper rates. Football season is here with all the colleges and high schools on board. One thing does not change. Wine is still in season all year.

I have recently discovered a new foodee love, raw oysters on the half shell and have been writing about it a lot, but it deserves attention, because like wine consumed responsibly, they are very healthy for you. They contain very little fat, lots of iron as well as Omega-3 fatty acids. They are a perfect pairing with a good white wine. Wait a minute. I just intimated that wine is good for you. Of course oysters are good for you because they are seafood and we all know the benefits of seafood. But wine? That is what makes you flighty as a bird or courageous as a lion. The worst scenario is one may have the demeanor of a jack ass.

Yes, wine is good for you. My wife teases me about my sensitive stomach, but as Paul wrote in the New Testament, "a little wine is good for digestion." That is not merely a good thing because it is written in the Scriptures, I have found it to be very true. My recommendation is that a glass of red wine a day, as it really does aid digestion.

I have spoken to a number of people who are told by their doctor to drink a glass of red wine for their heart. Wine has been noted by nutritional researchers to actually help prevent clotting of blood in the arteries because it causes the red blood cells to separate instead of grouping together and clogging blood vessels.

My favorite reason for drinking wine has nothing to do with health or oysters. I enjoy wine, particularly as it enhances a meal. It is the only drink that can enhance food whether fast food or a heavy holiday meal. Try a good French rosé from the

Côte de Rhone the next time you have a pizza or a sausage hot dog. It is nothing short of wonderful, raising the level of a convenience food to an enjoyment one would not have imagined.

Of course, that is not to take away from the obvious pallet delight of a bold red with a large meal. All to say, wine needs to be de-mystified in our culture. It is an excellent beverage not just because of its taste and health benefit, but also because of its versatility with food.

For those of you who want to try a white wine with oysters on the half shell or however they are prepared, I recommend a good *Piquepoule* from the Languedoc region of France.

Enjoy!

THE WINES OF ARGENTINA
November, 2009

I

What a difference time can make in one's viewpoint. One year ago, all I knew of Argentina was that Malbec had finally found a home there and was thriving. Since then I have done some research and have discovered quite a history of the blend of wine and politics that has proven to be fascinating. In today's market, Argentina has grown to be the fifth largest wine producer in the world behind France, Italy, Spain and the USA, but that is not how it all began.

By 1556, Spanish priests brought vines (most likely a Criola Grande varietal) across the Andes mountains into Chile to be planted for the production of wine for communion. With the establishment of vineyards in Mendoza by the end of the sixteenth century, the wines continued to develop to such a degree that by the eighteenth century that they were well known throughout the area and were a major domestic trade product. In the 1880's a French botanist introduced French varietal vines that did very well in the Mendoza area. As Italian and Spanish winemakers immigrated into Mendoza, they brought with them their native vines which grew equally as well as the French vines.

The most well known of the European varietals to thrive in the Mendoza region has been Malbec. One of the five Bordeaux varietals, by the time Malbec arrived in Argentina, it had been sent to Spain and Portugal in an attempt to find a place where it could thrive, with no results even moderately comparable to the growth and development achieved in Mendoza.

What made this varietal such a success in an arid, dry area such as Argentina? One must look at the characteristics of the grape itself to answer the questions concerning its European migration leading to the immigration to Mendoza. The Malbec grape is very susceptible to rot and mildew, both of which are very prevalent under normal conditions in many areas of Europe. Upon arrival in Argentina where there is almost no rain, rot and mildew became of little concern to vine growers in the region. With hail being the main worry, vineyards were soon spread out to minimize the effects.

Given the natural proclivity the Mendoza region provided for the European vidias vinefera, there would seem that there is nothing that could thwart the growth and development of wine production. The geological, political and economic factors have had great affect on this burgeoning industry.

II

Looking at the wine industry in Argentina today, one would never know what a difficult rise to world prominence it had to go through. Considering the conditions for growing grapes in Argentina, it should be noted that the general climate is very arid and dry. Not just dry, but really dry. According to the BBC, the average rainfall is less than 200 millimeters with a humidity that varies between forty to seventy percent. With the main source of water for the Mendoza River being the spring run off of the snow melting from the heights of the Andes mountains., how did the Mendoza area become such a fertile zone? The answer lies in the history of Argentina prior to the arrival of the Spanish.

Before the Spanish came, the Mendoza area was populated by the Huarpes Indians, said to be part of the Incan empire. By the time the Spanish arrived, the Incas had been so decimated that there was little sign of their rule in the area. All that was left was an advanced irrigation system that controlled the flow of water through channels from the Mendoza River causing the dry arid region to be an excellent growing area.

19

Although much more advanced (and expensive) methods of irrigation are starting to find their ways into the agricultural industry of the Mendoza region, the slightly modified Huarpes irrigation system is still in use today.

The immigration of both Spanish and Italians in the late 1800's added to a culture where wine was found at every meal. On a world wide scale, the Argentines drink much more than anyone else. During the 1970's and 80's the consumption of wine fell off as the wine industry was attempting to grow. This caused an over production of wine that the government of Argentina tried to stop by artificially supporting the co-ops and vineyards; a plan that met with disastrous results. Even with the purchase of many wine producing lands by the government and large corporations, everything eventually collapsed leaving abandoned vineyards across the Mendoza region. Deregulation of the vineyards in the 1990's caused a much stronger growth of the industry including much higher quality.

The dilemma that faced wine producers at this point was the diversity between the domestic and international markets. Hoping to develop the international market called for the investments of Europeans, but until the investments were made, the domestic market was what really kept the industry afloat. Local wine drinkers were used to drinking lower quality "table wines" while the quality the international market demanded was much higher. For those vineyards large enough, it was merely a question of making two different wines, while the smaller vineyards had to gradually increase the quality of their wines so as not to lose the domestic customers while attracting the European and other international markets. The very smallest vineyards were forced to choose which market they were going to serve. As can be readily seen, the advance of the wine market from Argentina has been no small accomplishment.

III

The wines of Argentina, both from a historic and a geo-political viewpoint, has proven to be a most interesting and fascinating study. Whatever the past, the proof of the validity of the Argentinian wine industry is no more evident than in the varietals produced currently.

The most well known of the Argentine varietals is the Malbec. Although the popularity of Malbec has only in recent years climbed into the forefront of the wine industry, the varietal has been developed over the last one hundred years in Mendoza next to the Andes mountains. With a small, dark and juicy fruit, the degree of reliance on irrigation allows growers the ability to control the quality of the fruit. In some of the higher altitudes around Mendoza, it has a thick skin with high tannins and acidity, making for a robust wine; while in the lower climates the thinner skin grapes are juicer making for lighter wines. Because of the ample use of oak, Malbec often carries the flavors of vanilla, spice, and some tobacco flavors.

With the Italian immigration of the 1890's into Argentina came the Bonarda Piomentese varietal of grape from the Piedmont region of Italy. A very prolific grape in the Argentine climate, it was the most widely planted grape until Malbec took its place. One of the last grapes to be harvested, the Bonarda grape produces a wine that is light and fruity with cherry and plum flavors, having light tannins and medium acidity.

Tempranillo, a native varietal from northern Spain, produces a light bodied wine due to its low acidity and low sugar. Because it is lighter bodied, it is often used for blending, typically with Garnacha in Rioja. The Argentine use of oak in aging this wine gives a dark fruited flavor with lots of plum, and shades of vanilla and spice. Due to its sensitivity, Tempranillo does very well in cooler areas with water management, which makes it an excellent varietal for the areas around Mendoza. Because it ripens early, it does not require a long growing season making it all the more versatile.

One of my favorite varietals, Sangiovese, is best known as a basis for the many Tuscan blends such as Chianti and Brunello di Montalcino. Because of its acidity, it ages very well, developing a medium fruit flavor and often has a very dry finish. Like Tempranillo, Sangiovese is an early ripening varietal in the Mendozan climate as opposed to other areas where it ripens fairly late. The few vintners who use the Sangiovese are those who are very prestigious in the Argentine wine industry using their wines mostly in the export markets.

Among the many other varietals grown in Argentina are those more familiar Cabernet Sauvignon, Merlot, and Syrah. Argentina is not just a haven for wines that have not made it as a single varietal in other countries, it is a treasure that is just being discovered. Awaiting the next period of time in this wonderful history are wine lovers everywhere that have only in the last one hundred years come to appreciate what lies at the foot of the Andes Mountains.

WINE AND NUTRITION
October, 2009

Recently I was asked to help someone choose a wine that would help them build up their blood because they had heard that it was necessary to drink a glass of wine for their health. This falls right in line with many comments I hear about using wine as an agent of good health. To assist me in answering some of the myths and facts concerning wine and health, I consulted Carl Raezstch, a friend who has two bachelors degrees (genetics and biochemistry) from Texas A and M and a masters degree in nutritional microbiology from the University of North Carolina. I guess that makes him as much of an expert as I need.

Moderate consumption of alcohol is said to be good for one's health with red wine being the most recommended. On the other hand (and I hate to have to say this but feel it necessary), it should be noted that excessive amounts do not do excessive amounts of good. One to three glasses of wine are considered to be moderate amounts on a daily basis. With moderate consumption of red wine, studies have shown an affect on several areas of one's health: longevity, and a decrease in heart disease, cholesterol, and cancer.

The substance resveratrol is in the skin of grapes and is transferred to the wine during fermentation. Only red wines are fermented with the skins which causes the color to be red. When resveratrol was given to mice, it was found not only did the mice live longer, but they also were found to have a lower incidence of cancer.

The decrease of heart disease is said to be very difficult to ascertain in mice, however there is a cultural study that tends to support this. In France, where wine is a staple, there is little heart disease despite an average diet that is reportedly one of the worst. Add to that the excessive use of tobacco, and a 'cardio-paradox' is produced that can be one proof of the decrease of heart disease with moderate red wine consumption. Another study shows that red wine makes red platelets less adhesive to each other and to the walls of blood vessels. This effect usually lasts approximately two days, so the daily consumption of red wine causes an extension of this effect, lowering the chances of higher cholesterol.

It should be noted that wine in any amount is not a magic potion. Just as vitamin tablets cannot be considered as good nutrition, there is nothing in wine that can replace proper diet and exercise in order to insure good health. As always, it has been my contention that wine is to be enjoyed, so good health is just icing on the cake (diet?).

Cheers to your good health!

THE HISTORY OF WINE IN VIRGINIA
October, 2009

In 2007 we celebrated the 400th anniversary of the the founding of Jamestown, the first permanent English settlement in North America. A little known fact remains that 2007 also marks 400 years of wine production in Virginia.

The first attempts at producing wine were met with disaster. Although wine was made from native grapes, the wine was totally unacceptable and vines from Europe were imported into the colony. Wine was to be the original cash crop from Virginia with the potential thought to be so great that in 1619 a law was enacted that required every male colonist to plant and maintain a minimum of ten vines or pay a penalty in corn. As soon was found, the phylloxera infestation which attacked the vitas vinefera from Europe, caused the corn coffers to be full and the wine casks to remain empty. The potential for wine to be a cash crop was supplanted by the rapid growth in trade of another crop, tobacco. As interest in wine waned, the development of tobacco as Virginia's cash crop burgeoned.

Throughout the history of Virginia attempts were made to develop European grape vines for wine production. The most famous was by Thomas Jefferson who experimented at Monticello for some thirty years yet never produced a single drop of wine. A contemporary, George Washington, tried to develop vines at Mount Vernon for eleven years, achieving the same results as Jefferson.

In the early 1800's the emphasis turned back to vines native to North America with much success. The Norton grape, discovered on Belle Isle in Richmond, Virginia by Dr. Norton, for whom the grape is named, became world famous in 1873 at the World's Fair in Vienna when a Norton wine was named "best red wine of all nations." At the Paris World's Fair when the

Eiffel Tower was constructed, a Virginia Norton wine won a gold medal. The discovery that would ultimately be ingrained into the psyche of vintners everywhere was when the root stock from North American vines could be grafted on to European stock, a disease and pest resistant strain was produced. This discovery was the saving grace when the phylloxera destroyed many of the vines of Europe and did much to bolster the wine industry in Virginia until early in the twentieth century.

The first part of the twentieth century brought Prohibition and set back wine production in Virginia to such a degree that we were almost in the twenty first century before we finally began to recover from it. Almost twenty years after the repeal of Prohibition saw only fifteen acres of land in use for commercial wine making.

With experimentation with European stock leading the way in the 1950's, a true resurgence began in vineyards planted in the 1970's. One of the first major vineyards to appear was the work of Italian Gianni Zonin when he hired Gabriele Rouse and established the Barboursville vineyards near Charlottesville. Growth came rapidly to the Old Dominion with forty six vineyards being in operation by 1995 and one hundred seven by 2005. At present, there are more than two hundred fifty vineyards in Virginia with more being planned. Today, Virginia wines are finding approval not only in this country, but in countries all over the world. From difficult beginnings, the wine industry in Virginia has overcome much and is well on its way to becoming the cash crop it was expected to be in the beginning at Jamestown in 1607.

A SUMMER WINE COLUMN
June, 2008

I never liked the beach and have always wondered why people flock there and eat sand and suntan lotion for a week or however long they are able to tell themselves they are having fun.

Having grown up camping in the mountains and gone to college in the Shenandoah Valley, sifting sand never had much of an appeal to me. Give me a cool mountain stream any day; at least you can see the other side.

As close as I would want to go to the beach would be the Northern Neck, which is close enough to get the wonderful seafood (my only consolation for ever going to the beach), but not overrun by a tourist population competing with lobsters for a reddish hue.

The number of wineries in the Northern Neck has grown and continue to grow. This area of the Commonwealth is said to be Bordeaux like because of its climate, and offer a wide variety of wines which meet even the most peevish of pallets. Virginians are starting to get into the white wines as wineries are introducing wines such Vidal Blanc and Chardonnays that are aged in stainless steel. Add to this wine region the proximity of the Virginia Oyster Trail, and the attraction is matchless. The best part of it all is no sand.

With the advent of the hot weather that has descended upon us, many think of "summer wines." I have no problem with these wines except when people try to match them with meals that do not pair well, no matter how good the wine is. For those who would like a change, the white Bordeaux has been on the market for several years and stands to edge out the New Zealand grapefruit bombs. A crisp, clean taste entices the tongue to savor as the flavor spreads throughout the pallet. Light, but bold, this wine is excellent for those raw oysters found along the Rappahannock River near Topping. The wine goes perfect with the sweet, mineralization found in such shell fish. If you prefer, roast the oysters, they pair well with wine also.

In the Loire River Valley, next to the town of Tours in France is the area of Vouvray. Here wines are so luscious, neighboring areas have made the news recently for trying to copy them and use the name to attract attention. Aged in stainless steel, this fine wine delivers a fruitiness that goes well solo or with heavy hors-d'oeuvres. Like the white Bordeaux, it goes very well with seafood.

One of my favorites for the summer remains a dry Rose from the Cote de Rhone area in southeast France. Based on the Grenache grape, Syrah and Mouvedre add just the right touch to make this wine exciting. A Sicilian cohort of mine recently introduced me to the Italian version known as a Rosatto. Made from Sangiovese, the addition of Merlot adds body and a darker color. The use of Vidal Blanc gives the wine a light touch.

Because both Rose and Rosatto are not left on the grape skins long before they are pressed they end up with a pink color and many mistake them for a blush. Brrrrrr! That makes my blood run cold. This is a completely different animal and should be treated as such. It can easily be drunk in both winter and summer.

Whatever you drink, please enjoy, and please drink responsibly.

Cheers!

THE DOG DAYS OF AUGUST
August, 2008

We are at the time of the summer we used to call, "the dog days of August" when growing up in Central Virginia, because the temperature averaged ninety degrees or more with high humidity. I remember helping my father run wire for a special plug in order to use our window air conditioner (the first on the block). There was no central air conditioning and everyone would sit and sweat. Now air conditioning is required by all or a national emergency is declared. Other than the weekly homemade ice cream with the Masons next door, no one felt like eating much.

Maybe this is a throw back to former times, but I eat noticeably less this time of year. My schedule used to keep me away from home for supper and I discovered eating healthy (no kidding, folks) in the evening. A favorite snack was hummus with crackers and/or fruit. There are many good wines that go well with summer snacks or light suppers served late in the day.

I had finished bottling my latest batch of red wine, a Bordeaux mix of Cabernet Sauvignon, Cabernet Franc, and Merlot and found that with the strong flavors of hummus (I use plenty of garlic and hot sauce), the big Bordeaux pairs very well. Reds are not solely for winter and whites for summer; toss the rules and drink what you will. When a less dominant wine is preferred, I would recommend a rose (not to be confused with a blush or white zinfandel). A good rose is refreshing to the palette as well as being a wine able to stand up to a variety of foods.

Happy Dog Days!

My hummus recipe goes well with both a good summer or winter wine. Here it is:

INGREDIENTS
2 -15 ½ oz cans of chick peas, drained and rinsed
¼ cup lime juice
Garlic cloves (as many as you can stand)
2 tbsp Tahini (sesame paste)
2 tbsp chopped parsley
1½ tsp cumin
½ tsp coriander
1½ tsp soy sauce
Ground red pepper and /or hot pepper sauce
Salt and fresh ground pepper

DIRECTIONS
Puree all ingredients in a blender or food processor. If too thick, add small amounts of olive oil or water and reprocess until desired consistency is reached.

PB&J AND MALBEC
July, 2012

I never thought of myself as an artist until I was in college, and then only at the suggestion of a friend of mine one day as we were eating lunch in the dining hall. As was my tendency then and to some degree even now, I was making a peanut butter and jelly sandwich.

The observant coed exclaimed to me in the middle of my preparation,"Scott, you are an artist, no one takes such care in making a peanut butter and jelly sandwich!"

Please note that growing up eating this wonderful bit of Americana, I had developed my own style of making it, in addition to the fact that I have seen many incorrect ways that send shudders down my spine.

First of all, both pieces of the bread need to be laid flat on whatever surface is being used, whether a counter top or a plate. Secondly, the order of application is most important with peanut butter being spread on the left piece of bread with a full spread application. Depositing a glob of peanut butter in the middle of the bread and being too lazy to spread it out is just gross. A little work never hurt anyone, so spread it to the far reaches of the the crust (please leave the crust on), leaving no part of the upper side of the bread exposed. The same applies to the jelly, applied to the right piece of bread. There is no kind of jelly that one must use, but for this article, I would say use Concord grape. Again, a little work spreading works wonders for this sandwich, so do not fall into the trap that many do of mixing both on the same piece of bread (even worse are those premixed jars). The jellied bread always goes on top of the other bread and is plated so that when one picks up the sandwich and bites into it, the jelly is on top.

This takes practice so do not be disappointed if at first it does not seem to work out well. One of the great things about the practice of making these sandwiches is eating your mistakes.

Of course, as a child, I was given milk with my sandwich, but I am no longer a child so I have found something that goes with it equally as well, and even though many think I am merely kidding, I am actually quite serious. My drink of choice with a peanut butter and jelly sandwich is none other than a good, rich glass of Malbec. I am sure the French had no idea of this kind of pairing when developing this wine. Now that it is made mostly in Argentina, a new world country, no holds are barred.

This is where the Concord grape comes into play. The jammyness of the jelly is offset by the rich fruit forwardness of the wine, with both flavors united by the taste of the peanut butter. While the sweetness of the jelly is pleasant to the end of one's tongue, the richness of a quality Malbec carries the entire experience into a transition to a moderate finish that is somewhat euphoric.

One must also understand the health aspects of this pairing. The protein in peanut butter is nothing but good. Used in moderate amounts, either crunchy or smooth are both excellent. While many may say that jelly is not the most healthy thing to eat, it is offset by the Malbec, a red wine, that is proven to be, in moderation, extremely healthy.

For the skeptics, I would encourage you to take this pairing and try it for yourself. I understand that some do not like peanut butter and jelly, and some do not like Malbec, but I promise you if you do like both, this is a delightful pairing guaranteed to bring even the haughtiest foodie culinary delight.

2009 NUGAN ESTATE SHIRAZ VISION REVERINA
August, 2011

Out of the Willbrigge area in the northern part of South West Australia comes a Shiraz unlike any that has been tasted for quite a while. The deep garnet color is as inviting as the nose of dark fruit and tar, with some oaking making its presence known. But how many wines have had this same promising bouquet only to disappoint the taster with a flat or tannic taste?

Nugan presents a Shiraz that is a balanced taste of dark plum, spice and chocolate, followed by a mid range of earthiness and concludes with a rather lengthy finish with just enough oak to wrap up the entire experience. Although there is a slight acidity, the overall taste is one of a very balanced, smooth texture.

While this wine would pair well with dark meats and large meals, the taste structure is such that it would also do well solo. This is one wine that should not be missed.

IT IS GETTING TO BE THAT TIME OF YEAR
June, 2010

By now, if you have not pulled out the grill or visited someone who has, undoubtedly the smell of a neighbor's outdoor culinary activities has greeted you at a time of venerability, that is, when you are most hungry. With the beginning of this season begins my crusade against what has become one of the most fallacious ideas our society can throw our way, the idea that summer is only for beer drinkers and those who insist on drinking those insipid single dimensional wines of summer that often plague us. For those who enjoy these beverages I mean no ill will. Instead I would like to advise there are many better than those wines that I consider one dimensional at a cost that is only nominally more.

As I am writing this, I have at my desk a bottle that will always be special to me, it is a rosé from the Cotes du Rhône, France by Cellier des Princes. It was my introduction to the true rosés of wine.   Unfortunately, because of its light appearance, many think of rosé as a blush or something akin to white zinfandel (Au contraire), the fact being this wine is a different animal altogether. Most of the rosés that come out of the Rhône area are made from a granache grape and blended with a syrah, resulting in a lovely initial taste filled with fruit that culminates throughout the tasting experience into a medium to long dry finish. The use of syrah adds just the right amount of velvet structure and spicy taste to make a rosé wine more than interesting.

My first experience with a rosé was one that I was sure would end in disaster. A hickory smoked pork tenderloin had been prepared very nicely when I discovered the only wine I had on hand was a French rosé. Much to my surprise (and relief), the wine paired with the pork very well, not only in taste, but also the structure of the wine made an extremely delightful complement to the entire meal.

And yet summer is not just about eating a grandiose grilled meal. My vision of the perfect summer is being outside, sitting back in a comfortable chair with some friends enjoying a refreshing glass of wine. Relaxation is a valuable endeavor not to be taken lightly, especially if good friends and tasty hors d'oeuvres are included. To match this standard I again refer to the Rhône area of France known as Pinet to enjoy Picpoul de Pinet (a Languedoc varietal). Served chilled, this refreshing white wine pairs well with mussels and other seafood fare and because of the lightly fruited taste that extends from the beginning until it is combined with a medium off dry finish, it can also be used with an appetizer or just by itself as an elegant patio wine.

Whenever quality summer wines are discussed, one should always remember the Loire River Valley in an area located adjacent to the eastern side of the town of Tours. Given a terroir of crushed limestone, sand and clay on a limestone base prevalent along the Loire River, wine makers Barton and Guesstier have produced what has become a favorite for many from this region known as Vouvray. Bearing the name of the area, B&G's Vouvray (as it is commonly known) is a medium bodied white wine that far exceeds the expectations of many. The initial full fruit flavor is merged in the middle with a judicious minerality that extends to a medium to full finish that is somewhat off dry, making it a wine that once tasted, it is not easily forgotten. Like the Picpoul, this is a wonderful wine with seafood or light poultry dishes, but continues to shine when drunk solo.

These three wines are quite moderately priced and represent a large number of wines that are available to each one of us at our local markets. Whether drinking a rosé, picpoul, vouvray, or any one of the many lovely wines of summer, enjoy.

MUSHROOM SOUP AND THE PHANTOM
December, 2009

In case you have not noticed lately, it is starting to get a bit nippy outside, with the temperature fluctuating from cold to warm, cool to hot, and then back to cold again. This is the time of year in Virginia when no one is quite sure what to wear outside and when the sales for tissues and handkerchiefs skyrocket. It is time to cook up a big pot of chicken soup for the soul, not to mention the nose, except for one thing – chicken soup has never done much for me when I have had a cold. I have discovered, instead, a soup that is going to be my soul pleaser and nose warmer for this year, and the only chicken in it is some chicken broth used in the preparation. Without further ado, please allow me to introduce:

Mushroom and Barley Soup
(Prevention Magazine, November 1999)

INGREDIENTS
1 oz dried mushrooms
1 1/2 tsp dried oregano
3 cups water
2 cans (14 1/2 oz ea) chicken broth
1 large onion, chopped
1/2 cup barley
2 carrots, chopped
1/2 tsp salt
1 celery rib, chopped
12 oz cremini or button mushrooms, Stemmed and sliced

DIRECTIONS

In a saucepan, bring dried mushrooms and water to a boil. Remove and let stand 15 min.

Coat a Dutch oven w/nonstick spray. Add onion, carrots, and celery. Coat lightly with nonstick spray. Cook over medium heat, stirring some for 3 min.

Add cremini mushrooms and oregano. Cook, stirring some, for 6-8 min or until vegetables are soft. Add broth, barley, and salt and cook for 10 minutes.

Line a mesh sieve with a coffee filter or paper towel and strain the dried mushroom water into the pot. Remove and discard the filter.

Rinse the dried mushrooms under running water to remove any grit. Chop the dried mushrooms and drop into the pot. Cook for 10-15 min or until the barley is tender.

As good as this soup is, what made it all the better for me was an accompanying wine I had with it. Every fall, Bogle Vineyards in California puts out a limited production of wine called the Phantom. This blend of petite syrah, old vine zinfandel and old vine mourvedre has become a cult favorite with many followers hounding wine shop keepers as to when the annual shipment of Phantom is going to arrive.

A strong red with a dark ruby color whose richness is matched only by the taste of dark fruit flavor with just the slightest hint of the well known zinfandel sweetness balanced by the spice coming from the petite syrah is immediately evidenced at the initial stages of tasting. The classic taste of the mourvedre rounds out the flavors in the mid range with a medium finish wrapping up the entire experience. It should be noted that the zinfandel and the mourvedre grapes in this wine are from old vines (approxiamately fifty to eighty years old) which, though they do not produce as much fruit, produce a very concentrated taste.

Now before all you carnivores turn your nose up at this dilectable feast, you need to try it. Granted, this is a vegetarian type of dish, however the mushrooms combined with the concentrate strained off the hydrated mushrooms gives it a meaty savor guaranteed to please even the most stringent of meat eaters.

For those of you who missed this year's installment of The Phantom, fear not, next year will hopefully bring another release just as good or better. Wine of this caliber brings me to my knees praying that the Lord of the Harvest blesses the fruit of the vines. Good wine with a soul pleasing soup makes one wonder, does it get much better than this? Bring on old man winter!

CAVA PERE VENTURA, BRUT NATURE
November, 2009

With the holidays approaching, everyone thinks of toasting the days with Champagne. And then the term sparkling wine rises to the surface. When I first heard the term "sparkling wine" many years ago, I thought it was an imitation of Champagne, to find later that sparkling wines produced in the French region of Champagne were the only ones that could be called Champagne. Champagne is, in fact, a sparkling wine.

Recently I procured a bottle of Cava Pere Ventura, Brut Nature. So then, what is Cava? It is the Spanish form of Champagne (Oops! Excuse me, I mean sparkling wine).

In 1872, Josep Raventós Fatjó of the Codorniu estate was the first in Spain to produce a wine in the Champagne method or "méthode champenoise" and was called cava after the cellars in which it was produced. It was soon to become very popular in particular with the elite and ruling classes.

Cava is made by first producing a white wine principally from the grapes from the Spanish native varietals Xarello, Macabeo, of Parellada. The second step is Tirajo in which the bottle is filled with blended wine and a syrupy mixture of yeast and sugars (licor de tirajo) causing a secondary fermentation in the temporarily corked bottle which lasts approximately nine months. During this time there is an occasional turning of the bottle (a process called remuage) to make the yeast residue settle in the neck of the bottle which is then frozen forcing the sediment out after which the bottle is then recorked.

For this tasting, drinking Pere Ventura, Cava Brut Nature (approxiamately $9-$12.00 for a 750 ml bottle), served as chilled as cold as possible (some insist on using a chilled glass) was a delight. The fine white bubbles preceded the lovely light wheat color which is the perfect invite to a holiday drink (or any other time). The initial taste produced a nice fruity taste that was matched only by a long dry finish carrying the initial taste throughout the entire experience. The effervescence kept my attention by continually enlivening my palate allowing me to be able to enjoy the long finish.

The lightness of this cava made it very refreshing and enjoyable. It was an excellent pairing for appetizers, however when tried with a slice of soprosetta salame on a Ritz cracker, it was unfortunately lost in the spice of the salame, with only the bubbles surviving, giving the impression that this cava may be best with a non spicy appetizer or some form of salad.

Whether as an apertif or just as a nice wine to enjoy with friends, Pere Ventura is an excellent wine to have in one's wine cellar. One word of advice: Do not drink this wine solely at the holidays or for special occasions. A cava like this can be enjoyed the entire year for any reason. If in fact you do use Cava Pere Ventura at a holiday gathering, toast in the Spanish tradition…

¡Próspero Año Nuevo!, to a Prosperous New Year!

BARBERA DEL MONFERRATO MINOLA
June, 2010

It is Saturday night and I am enjoying my favorite Saturday night pastime of watching a Netflix movie and drinking a glass of wine while my wife, Diane, works on ideas for the plans of our next house. With the weather outside being as cold as it is, the movie takes our minds off of the chill and the wine is a very delightful refreshment to accompany the evening.

This particular night I am enjoying a 2004 Barbera del Monferrato Minola produced by the Nuova Capaletta winery in Piedmont, Italy. The wine delivers a very fruitful first taste and has delightful finish that is complimented by the use of French oak in the aging process. A very full bodied wine, it is one that can be paired with a substantial meal as well as being drunk by itself. This wine is from the Minola vineyard near the Vignale Monferrato municipality

The grapes for this wine are picked by hand and fermented for about two weeks and then after being filtered, is placed in French oak barrels to be aged for a period of one year. After bottling, the wine is then aged in the estate cellar for six months.

What peaked my interest about this wine is that the Nuova Capaletta farm (which includes the winery) is completely organic. Registered organic since 1986, the new term for this type of farming is biodynamic agriculture, which refers to a type of management in which the land is agri-managed for sustainability, with all activities interrelated. The goal of this type of land management is to not use chemicals and to be more aware of cultivation so as to increase and preserve land fertility. At Nuova Capaletta, the farm is seen as a living organism, not just a piece of land where plants are grown; every part of it affecting the other. The extension of this philosophy is that we are all tied in together affecting one another by what we do.

Biodynamic agriculture is part of a chain reaction of various individuals that includes not only the farmer, but also those processing the product, distributors and the retailers who finally sell to the consumer what is supposed to be a not only a heartier, more flavorful product, but supposedly a more healthy one.

BOY NEEDS TO MEET WINE, NOT JUST GRILL
June, 2011

Even though summer just began June 21, the grilling season has been with us for some time now.   If there is doubt, just look in all the life style magazines. Grilling and outdoor parties have been the main topic for the last two to three months showing us everything from how to make the most awe inspiring cole slaws to the expertly grilled hot dogs.   Of course, paper plates are not white anymore, they have to color coordinate with the napkin and cup in a pattern that hides the three bean salad that gets dumped on plates despite protests.

There is one thing about the grilling that makes it the highlight of the summer, that being the wine that accompanies all these dishes. Neither wine nor food is made to stand out, but instead accompany one another making a harmonious blend of culinary delight. Despite the heat of summer when light to medium bodied whites are the rage, they do not have that same taste that seems to fit so well with a steak or a pork loin, or what ever comes off of the grill. And while I will hold to my ideal that everyone should drink what they like, a good red wine does something for me in my relationship with grilled food no white will ever do.

Let us at this point be more specific. When it comes to grilling, the red of choice for the past several years has been, and still is, Zinfandel. A full bodied red wine with a hint of sweetness that makes it markedly different from Cabernet Sauvignon, Zinfandel was made for grilled meats with its taste of dark fruit and spice that is followed by a long finish, aged in a judicious amount of both French and American oak. It has become a major component in what is considered by many to be the art of outdoor cooking.

A Zin that sits atop many good wine lists is 2008 Cline's Ancient Vine Zinfandel ($12.99 in some stores), a wine that almost defies description. The vines themselves are approximately eighty to one hundred years old or more and produce only a small amount of fruit, but with a very concentrated flavor. Cline takes this concentration and turns it into very deep, spicy richness that excites the senses and brings the grilled product into a world of sophistication all its own.

Just when the standard has been set, along come the Argentinians with their Malbecs. After several years of not having to worry about what to serve when grilling, this wine has arrived with a depth of character never before imagined from a non European wine. Running a close second behind Zinfandels, Malbec offers a new and exciting twist on the harmony everyone hopes to arrive at when pairing wine with grilled foods.

Case in point being the 2007 Trinchero Golden Harvest Malbec which was presented to me recently as a gift from my daughter, Emily. After allowing it to breathe for about thirty to forty minutes, the taste blossomed into a smoky, dark fruit phenomenon where not only was the fruit prevalent, but also the presence of the land from which the grapes were grown was blended in for an experience that could only be described as magnificent. There was not enough wine in the bottle to make it last until the next grilling, however the components were there that pointed to this wine being an excellent pairing for a meal fresh off the grill.

Whether or not it proves to be true, grilling in the summer has all the indications of taking a major turn with not only the development of more sophisticated Zinfandels, but also the addition of some of Argentina's best: Malbec.

SANGRIA: THE SPANISH LADY OF THE BARBECUE
August, 2009

Believe it or not it is summer with all the activities and stuff that goes with it. We have had our share of heat, lawn mowing (which has been easier at times thanks to my neighbor forcing me to use his riding mower) and farmer's markets with all the wonderful fresh produce. But sometimes I seem to forget how special this season can be until something awakens me and I see what it is all about.

This past Sunday the Richards clan all gathered at my son Kyle's house in Richmond for a cookout that made memories of of summer foods that I know will last quite a while.

Kyle's Ashley made a magnificent spread as she is want to but of course everyone else brought something as well ,which by the end of the day made us all rather full. My wife, Diane, brought her classic and most excellent potato salad, putting me in a bind as to what sort of drink to bring.

I really put myself on the chopping block by telling Kyle I was making Sangria. From the time I confirmed I was making it until the actual cookout, he called quite a few times to tell me how excited he was that I was bringing the Sangria. Dad had to come through on this one.

As it turned out, it was very good so I wanted to share the recipe, but one needs to look at the wine that went into this recipe.

Sangria, being a fruity drink, should have a fruity wine with some complexity of taste that makes a good addition but does not overpower. This, of course, is the description of many Spanish wines, which are among my favorites. For the Sangria, I used 2005 Coloma Garnacha Rioja, which with its upfront strawberry and cherry flavor melding into a midrange of cherry and a dry, tannic finish was perfect.

Here is the recipe. Note this is not overly sweet Sangria as this has the fruit taste with the dry finish for a very refreshing, drink.

INGREDIENTS
2 bottles fruity wine
2 oranges cut into slices
2 limes cut into slices
2 cups orange juice
2 cups lemonade
2 cups pomegranate/blueberry juice
Sugar as needed (I used about a cup)

DIRECTIONS
In a large bowl, add the wine and the fruit (minus seeds if possible), squeezing the fruit slices in half to incorporate the juices. Add the juices and sugar and stir, then refrigerate overnight to allow the flavors to come together. In addition to the wine, some have been known to add cognac to enhance the flavor.

This recipe can be easily halved or doubled and is super easy to make. **One note of caution**: There is alcohol in this drink but it does not taste like it. Please be careful and drink responsibly. I pray your outings are safe and enjoyable.

BAREFEET AND YELLOW TAILS
August, 2009

I do not mean to offend anyone's sensibilities, but sometimes things in life appear to me as funny in a different sort of way and I find my reaction to be just aside of the norm. Recently as I was perusing a large wine store, I was struck by some of the names that appeared on wine labels. We all know that beer and ale companies have gone totally crazy with many of their titles, but I thought wine would remain a stalwart against all of that madness. It is completely the fault of the Aussie exports into this country.

Who would have thought that any one would have nerve enough to export the quality of wine in the quantities they did and then turn around and try to draw attention to it? Why not call it by the common varietal name like Australian Merlot in order to hide it, but no, these people are serious – Yellow Tail. It reminds me of when my daughter Emily was young, we got a cat and she wanted to name it "Yellow Dog." Thank goodness that did not catch on, but after all, it was just one cat. The Australians have flooded our market with this stuff.

To make things worse, the west coast has decided to join the bandwagon with their wines known as Barefoot. I am not sure whether these nomenclatures are descriptions of the wines or not, but one thing is certain, it makes for excellent marketing because both the Aussie and the west coast wines are selling like hot cakes, and it has not stopped. Several years ago a neighbor gave me a glass of wine called Red Truck. Since then I have seen White Truck and Pink Truck. I am sure you can find them parked in front of, or at least near to the wines Big House White, Big House Red, and Big House Pink. That must be some neighborhood.

Not only have our neighborhoods come under attack, but

as well, the sanctity of our families is now being reviled. The wine Mad Housewife contains a narrative on the back of the bottle describing a woman who has gone mad with all her house work and now is content to curl up in the laundry room with her bottle of wine. The bottle of Old Fart wine gives us an opportunity to laugh about the similarities between geriatrics and the aging of wine while drinking a French blend. Marilyn Monroe Merlot wine, with a picture of the diva herself on the front, allows us to posthumously keep her memory in mind while the wine itself does whatever it can to our insides.

There is one wine at which I will poke no fun, known as Jar Head Red. The proceeds from the sale go towards the education of those children whose parents have fallen while on duty with the Marine Corps. Since this piece was originally written, I have had the opportunity to taste Jar Head Red and can say with all honesty that this is a red blend worth trying. Coming across with a bold, dark fruit flavor, the finish is inviting and of medium length and goes well with meats and casseroles.

As I have often written, drink what you like, but do not be confused by the hilarity of the labels you may see. As often as possible, go to a tasting and try different wines, it is a lot less expensive than buying a bottle of something that gets poured down the drain.

A ROSÉ IS NOT A BLUSH
July, 2014

The Virginia wine industry needs to be congratulated on its advancement in many areas. However, probably the most pronounced difference between now and twenty five years ago is the development of the Rosé wines.

When I was first exploring Virginia wines, I was at a function where a "rosé" was being served from a local winery. My first taste of the wine made me think I would never touch another wine from this state. What was touted to be a rosé, was in fact more of a blush, and not a very good one. Thankfully, I have been introduced to the real deal and am quite a fan.

The process of making a true rosé involves more than just having a pink wine. In the Côte de Rhone region of France, where the true rosé was first developed, one of the major grapes used is the Grenache. The body of the wine is far from what blush drinkers experience. Because of its elegance, Syrah is often added to the Grenache and topped off with something like Mouvedre that will allow the wine to have a depth that can be surprising to the novice rosé drinker.

I will never forget my first bottle of this wine. All I had to eat with it was a piece of hickory smoked pork loin. Looking at the wine, with its light color and knowing what kind of taste the pork had, I was sure the taste of the rosé would be lost.

Much to my surprise, the wine not only held up to the taste of the pork, it matched it perfectly! Since that time, I have had the pleasure of tasting many differing rosés, and have yet to be disappointed.

Of course, the Italians are not to be outdone. I raise Sangiovese in my vineyard and I am salivating at the prospect this spring of making a Rosatto (an Italian rosé). Again, the grape used in this wine will be one of character and strength as is that used in the French version, but with a decided different taste due not only to the grape, but to the development of the wine as well.

Because the color of the wine is due almost wholly to the contact with the skins during fermentation, a rosé is taken off of the skins after several days, thus having a much lighter hue. One of the big differences I have found between a rosé and a blush is that a rosé is much drier. The character of the rosé allows it to be used as an excellent patio wine, or as a wine that can be used with many different types of food. The example of the hickory smoked pork loin is a good example.

In my bar tending days, I used to cringe at mixing what one customer called a White Zin Spritzer, a mixture of white zinfandel (blush) and ginger ale. But, as I always say, drink what you like.

THANKSGIVING WINES 2012
November, 2012

It is that time of year again when we start thinking about everyone getting together and being nice to each other for a few short hours around the Thanksgiving table. I have discovered that is much more pleasant with a good wine to accompany the meal. Easier said than done.

The problem I have run into in the past has been the plethora of flavors that is on the table and having wine to match them. That could get rather expensive, not to mention intoxicating. One principle of pairing that I like to use which takes away a lot of the guess work is very simply *do not try to match the foods!* Now before all the foodies and wine snobs blackball me, hear me out.

The purpose of a pairing is not to have a wine that will taste good with the food or food that tastes good with the wine. The experience of pairing food and wine is one where neither the food nor the wine stands out but one is given the opportunity to accentuate the combination of both in order to experience and enjoy the flavor that results from the pairing.

I can think of two wines that I have used at my table in the past that have accomplished this very nicely. The first is Cline's Ancient Vine Zinfandel. The term ancient vine refers to the fact that the vines are about one hundred years or more in age. At this point, they do not produce as much fruit, but what they do produce is very concentrated in flavor. Cline has taken this grape and used it to produce a wine that not only pleases the palate with a concentration of dark berry flavors, but also gives off an richness and spice that absorbs into and blends with whatever else is your mouth (Thanksgiving dinner). The lingering finish is much like the beginning, very smooth and pleasing. The entire wine displays a lovely character that not only supports the army of food flavors attacking your tongue, but also adds an element of taste that enhances the flavor of whatever is on your plate. This is not a wine to be taken lightly, but to be enjoyed as a catalyst for elegance to your holiday fare and used to be found for less than $14.00 a bottle.

Of course, not everyone likes red wine. It is hard to imagine a white wine that would fit in this situation other than some oaky, buttery Chardonnay. Personally, I think butter should be reserved for Grandma Lynn's rolls to the degree that melted butter runs down your arm (please excuse my digression, but her rolls were always incredible). Getting back to wine, I have found that an off dry Riesling is an excellent choice for the occasion. Surprisingly, a good Riesling can carry the weight of a large meal such as Thanksgiving and one that I would recommend is Dr.L's Riesling, imported from Germany. This particular wine is not too sweet and not to dry, but is excellent in its good character and refreshing finish, in addition to allowing the drinker to enjoy the taste of the Riesling grape itself. And, one of the best parts is that it can be found at a decent price..

Another consideration might be a Super Tuscan. This is an Italian wine that is usually about eighty five percent Sangiovese and the remainder Cabernet Sauvignon and Merlot. Both of the latter wines are Bordeaux wines, therefore when they are added to Sangiovese, the resulting blend is referred to as a Super Tuscan.

Sangiovese, which is the main component for Chianti, is often fermented somewhat dry and has a lovely subdued dark cherry and fruit taste. Given the structure of the Cabernet Sauvignon and the roundness of the Merlot, a Super Tuscan would go very well with a holiday meal. It would go well with a hamburger, to be honest.

Of course, there is always Amarone, the prince of Italian reds. Made by drying the grapes prior to fermentation, this wine gives a concentrated taste that woos the palate with its silky texture and causes cessation to all activity as one sits in amazement that a wine could be so good. A wine that begs for good food, an Amarone by Allegrini goes for approximately $75-80.00 or more per bottle. It is worth every cent.

Whatever you drink, please enjoy responsibly and may the God of the Harvest bless you and your house abundantly.

ANOTHER SUMER WINE COLUMN
June, 2014

Anyone who writes about wine has written at one time or another how well white wine goes with summer and red wine with winter. In fact, as I was looking over past columns I have written for the Front Porch, I noticed that in June of 2013, I wrote a column titled,"The White Wines of Summer."

Getting older seems to have done more than just gray my hair. I have come to the conclusion that there are some absolutes that need to be abandoned. When it comes to drinking wine, the red-white seasonal thing is the first to go.

This has been a winter of whites at the Richards' household,. Not that reds have been ignored, mind you, but more whites have been drunk than usual. This is due largely to the fact that my father in law and daughter in law, both of whom are dear to me, are both white wine drinkers. Aside from the fact that he is from West Virginia and she is an ardent Green Bay Packers fan (and part owner), they both prefer white wines. Whenever there is a family gathering, whites have to be supplied.

At the mention of white wine, of course the first thing that comes to many people's mind is Chardonnay. Known primarily for its oaky, buttery taste, there is change even here. In the last number of years there has been a growing movement among Chardonnay drinkers who are tired of the oak taste and now it is not uncommon to find unoaked chardonnays. For those wines that are oaked, it is not as prevalent as it used to be. In America, oenologists are learning to use oak properly.

Pinot Grigio, an Italian unoaked wine that has found its way into the hearts and palates of many in the last several years, offers a tart, crisp semi fruit taste that is perfect for sipping solo, as is done often, or with a poultry or fish meal. Because it is not oaked, the clarity of flavor with a medium finish appeals to many, whether the outside is cold or warm.

The French counterpart, Pinot Gris, is a white wine aged in French oak. It should be indicated that French oak is very different from the American oak wine drinkers in the US are accustomed to. French oak provides a subtleness to the oaking that lends a hint of sweetness in the finish, more discerned than tasted.

Add this oaking to the Pinot Gris and one is transferred to a world of silky smoothness of the taste of the fruit. Like Pinot Grigio, Pinot Gris pairs well with fish and poultry. Both of these wines add to the coziness and comfort of a warm fire on a cold night accompanied by a plate hors d'oeuvres or tapas.

The use of Vidal Blanc adds another dimension to wine making and is becoming very prevalent in Virginia. Not only does it grow well, but also its taste as a finished wine is something not to be missed, no matter what the season.

Vidal Blanc offers a depth of character that goes beyond the fructose flavors one expects from whites. Often used in white blends, the Vidal Blanc flavor barely comes through, yet it adds a presence that lends a certain elegance to the finished product. A popular blend of this wine includes Viognier and Chardonnay. A lovely presentation, not too heavy, this wine goes well with shrimp or raw oysters. Rogers Ford Winery does an excellent job with this blend, calling it "Lily Grace" after wine founder John Puckett's granddaughter.

Wineries in Virginia have made some wonderful whites that really need to be tried. As I often tell people, drink what you like, but try Virginia wines. Also, bear in mind, one does not have to wait until the weather breaks this spring to try one of Virginia's fine white wines.

THREE SHADES OF ZIN
November, 2012

It got cold in Virginia recently. I must admit I get spoiled with the balmy weather, so when the cold strikes, I feel it. However, that does give an excellent opportunity to sit inside and sip on a glass of good wine.

Although the rules are thrown out concerning the seasons when we drink red or white, cold weather does give me an urge for a good red that is good by itself or with a hearty winter meal such as meatloaf and potatoes, or a comfort food such as chili.

The holidays always bring me in mind of zinfandel, usually an ancient vine zinfandel. Ancient vines are those that are at least eighty years old. The look like tree stumps in a field and because they are so massive, they are worked by hand. Although they do not produce as much fruit as a younger vine, the fruit is much better, making a better wine. Also popular are old vines, those thirty five to eighty years old. Although somewhat gnarly, these vines are more apt to be worked by machines, producing a grape that makes a wine not as mellow as the ancient vines

Most vintners and wine makers consider anything younger than an old vine, while it produce a nice wine, is not up to the quality of the older. In California, in the Alexander Valley, a new vine movement is under way. Douglas and Nancy Ousterhout purchased a winery out of foreclosure with zinfandel vines that were planted in 1999. Because the vines were neglected, they actually bought more of a mess of vegetation than a vineyard. With proper management, Nance's Winery, as it is now called, has produced two vintages of zinfandel in 2011 and 2012 that far surpass the norm. Instead of being a high alcoholic fruit bomb, they have made a very elegant and pristine wine.

Wine and Spirits magazine describes the 2011 Alexander Valley Nance's Vineyard Zinfandel as "...silky, delicate zin. It's as bright as a red cherry fresh off the tree, feeling almost weightless on palate. As the wine takes on air, the tannins provide an edgy minerality that focuses and amplifies the fruit into a sunny, ruby-red laser beam."

This is just one of the many zins coming out the west coast where zins grow best. In addition to chilis, this would be an excellent accompaniment to a light stew, or by itself in front of a fire on a cold night when the sound of the wind whipping around outside gives the ominous feeling of winter.

A good experiment would be to try all three types of zin. For the ancient vine, I wold recommend Cline's Ancient Vine Zinfandel. From the Napa Valley, the Elyse 2009 Black-Sears Vineyard Zinfandel, although a bit pricey is an excellent bottle.

My taste for zins comes and goes, but a good wine is a good wine. I cannot bring myself to be enough of a wine snob to follow any one wine over another. With that in mind, drink what you like as you sit in front of the fire with a bowl of warm stew or chili listening to the winter winds howl.

Cheers!

SHRIMP AND GRITS
September, 2015

The holidays are over now, most of the lights and tinsel are gone, except for those who leave their lights up all year. That also means the busy seasonal marathon of stuffing our faces with all kinds of food and abusing good wines has come to an end. This is soup season at the Richards' house, with everything from chicken soup to die for to some amazing chilis. Bear in mind these soups are homemade, with beans soaked overnight and vegetables cooked just right and served with Artisan bread slathered with butter. Although the temperature in Sparta, Virginia never gets too cold, the soup is wonderful when inside the warm house where no one has any idea what the temperature is outside. Pretending it is cold outside makes warm food taste all the better.

The other night Diane (wife, master soup maker) hit a new height when she made shrimp and grits. It could be said this is not a soup, but this was not just some shrimp thrown in with instant grits. We are talking about a broth made from the shrimp shells, bacon, tomato, dried peppers and a plethora of other good things in addition to the cooked grits and shrimp. The recipe used came from *The Joy of Cooking.*

A good soup makes for a wonderful meal, so why wash it down just with plain water? Soups beg for a good wine to pair with. Depending on the soup, the wine, as with any other food, varies.

As with many seafood dishes, shrimp and grits pairs best with white wine. In fact, red wine or any oaked wine should be avoided. The taste of this dish is harmonious and sophisticated and does not need to be hidden behind oaking or overpowered by a large red wine. Even a pinot noir would bring about too much of a contrast. Warm and delicious, this recipe needs room to fill

58

one's palate with flavors all their own. A white wine such as a *Chablis,* or a *White Bordeaux* offers a nice taste, without intruding on the integrity of the food, as they both meld their flavors into a wonderful pairing. Other wines to consider would be *a New Zealand Sauvignon Blanc* or *a Gruner Veltliner* from the area around Austria.

New Zealand is the home of *Brancott Sauvignon Blanc*, with its tropical flavors and intensely fresh taste make this one of two favorites to go with the shrimp and grits. Another is t*he 2011 vintage of Anton Bauer's Gruner Veltliner* with its lovely citrus notes of lemon, lime and grapefruit in the bouquet and minerality in the taste. The lower acidity of the wine makes it an excellent pairing.

Shrimp and grits with a good white wine is beyond amazing, and with the soup season has just starting, it looks like this winter is going to be warm and wonderful.

VOUVRAY
August, 2009

Too many times I find a wine I really like and do the research on it, only to set it aside and not touch it for a long time. Recently, while in a local wine store, I came across one of those long, lost loves.

I have always been a red wine drinker but will not turn down an excellent white, of which there are many. Barton and Guestier produce a chenin blanc out of the Loire River Valley in France that is extraordinary. In the eastern section, next to the town of Tours, lies an wine community known as Vouvray. The entire area is mostly limestone, and at this juncture of the Loire River, the soil has become, over the years, a mixture of gravel, sand and clay that adds an excellent mineralization to the wine produced there. The clay adds a unique flavor as well as nutrient base, while the sand and gravel are good for drainage in addition to the influence they have on the taste of the finished product.

The wine, known as Vouvray, is in fact, a chenin blanc, but is so named for the region it comes from. At first taste, one experiences a deep fruit on the palate that is supplemented by the a mineral flavor that shows off the terroir in which this wine is grown. Pear and fig strikes the palate immediately accompanied by the taste of sweet nuts rounding out a fruitiness with the slightest taste of citrus flavor. The mild acidity of this wine adds to its wonderful character, making for a pleasant mouthful of wine that needs to be chilled. The rule of thumb for chilling most whites is to serve it at approximately 50-55° F.

This wine has a rich but soft texture with a delightful finish and is best served with a light meal, but is excellent solo or with some light appetizers. The unique properties of this wine makes it one that can be served in the dead of winter in front of a fire or in the warmer spring and summer on the back deck prior to a cookout. One word is important to remember when partaking of a good Vouvray: Enjoy.

What better way to enjoy this wonderful wine than with a good plate of fish and chips made from the healthy haddock fish. Not only is it wonderful to the palate, it is healthy for the body.

The following recipe was taken from eatingwell.com:
<u>Oven Fried Fish and Chips From EatingWell:</u> **May/June 2009**.

Makes: 4 servings
Active Time: 25 minutes
Total Time: 45 minutes

INGREDIENTS
Canola or olive oil cooking spray
1 1/2 pounds russet potatoes, scrubbed and cut into 1/4-inch-thick wedges
4 teaspoons canola oil
1 1/2 teaspoons Cajun or Creole seasoning, divided
2 cups cornflakes
1/4 cup all-purpose flour
1/4 teaspoon salt
2 large egg whites, beaten
1 pound cod, (see Tip) or haddock, cut into 4 portions

DIRECTIONS
Position racks in upper and lower third of oven; preheat to 425°F. Coat a large baking sheet with cooking spray. Set a wire rack on another large baking sheet; coat with cooking spray.

Place potatoes in a colander. Thoroughly rinse with cold water, then pat dry completely with paper towels. Toss the potatoes, oil and 3/4 teaspoon Cajun (or Creole) seasoning in a large bowl. Spread on the baking sheet without the rack.

Bake on the lower oven rack, turning every 10 minutes, until tender and golden, 30 to 35 minutes.

Meanwhile, coarsely grind cornflakes in a food processor or blender or crush in a sealable plastic bag.

Transfer to a shallow dish. Place flour, the remaining 3/4 teaspoon Cajun (or Creole) seasoning and salt in another shallow dish and egg whites in a third shallow dish.

Dredge fish in the flour mixture, dip it in egg white and then coat all sides with the ground cornflakes.

Place on the prepared wire rack. Coat both sides of the breaded fish with cooking spray.

Bake the fish on the upper oven rack until opaque in the center and the breading is golden brown and crisp, about 20 minutes.

Tips & Notes

Tip: Overfishing and trawling have drastically reduced the number of cod in the U.S. and Canadian Atlantic Ocean and destroyed its sea floor. For sustainably fished cod, choose U.S. Pacific cod or Atlantic cod from Iceland and the northeast Arctic. For more information, visit Monterey Bay Aquarium Seafood Watch at seafoodwatch.org.

Nutrition: Per serving: 325 calories; 5 g fat (0 g sat, 3 g mono); 43 mg cholesterol; 45 g carbohydrates; 0 g added sugars; 24 g protein; 3 g fiber; 331 mg sodium; 955 mg potassium.

Nutrition Bonus: Vitamin C (58% daily value), Potassium (27% dv).   Carbohydrate Servings: 3

VINES

FLOYD
October 2015

In 2009, while embarking on a career as a pharmacy tech that I thought would be have some future, I found my self working retail in the wine business for Wegman's Market. Although I never was able to secure employment in the pharmacy business, my experience in wine retail proved to be invaluable.

Prior to opening the store for business, the entire wine department took a field trip to Ingleside Winery in Westmoreland County to tour the winery and speak with the winemaker there. In addition to the winemaker, we also met the individual in charge of the vineyard, who seemed at the time to be very quiet and nondescript.

After the grand opening of the store I was working and went to wait on a customer who was wearing a shirt with a wine statement on it. I made a comment about the shirt as part of relating to the customer, and he immediately responded that I should know him, we met at Ingleside. Lo and behold, this was the quiet, nondescript vineyard superintendent! Not as quiet, and with a smile that covered three counties, I found Floyd Oslin to be an extremely gregarious individual who had an infectious passion for wine.

Originally from Bangor, Pennsylvania, in the upper end of the Lehigh Valley, Floyd Oslin has been in the wine business since the age of sixteen.

Oslin's paternal grandfather owned a merchant fleet in Sicily, but sold it to come to America. Arriving with a large nest egg, the elder Oslin was quite the entrepreneur, peddling homemade wine, fruit from his orchard, and produce. When the winter months hit, he had a sawmill from which came most of the timbers used in local mines.

Oslin stated he remembers sitting on the basement steps watching his grandfather, father and uncles making wine. Dego Red, using Zinfandel, Alaconte, and Moscato was made in September in such a way that it was available by Christmas. By the next September, the two sixty gallon barrels of wine that had been made were gone. At the age of sixteen, Oslin began making wine, and at eighteen, the entire operation was turned over to Oslin.

One of his early influences came from Sid Butler, an engineering professor at Lehigh University, who owned the Slate Quarry Winery. Working there, Oslin commented that a light bulb went off in his head that this might really be the job he was looking for. Oslin continued his education in wine working for Franklin Hill Winery owned by Charles Flat. At Shumaker Orchard, he planted the vineyard.

An automobile accident left him the hospital for three and one half months, where Oslin said he did a lot of soul searching and made the decision to pursue oenology and viticulture full time.

His grandfather encouraged him, saying, "Get away from here. Find your passion and pursue it."

After sending his resume to many wineries including Treville Lawrence. Lawrence, of the Virginia Vineyards Association (VVA), sent Oslin's resume to Doug Flemer of Ingleside Vineyards.

October of 1982 was one of the turning points for him when he entered the Albemarle Wine Festival with two hybrid variety wines, winning first place. At the time there were only five or six wineries in the state and Oslin drew the attention of both the owner of the Barboursville Winery and Jim Livingston, who now owns Hartwood Winery.

He landed at Ingleside Winery in June, 1983, where he worked under Dr. Jacques Recht. At a VVA meeting in July, 1983, Oslin was introduced to Livingston, a relationship that continues to this day.

"Jim has been like a father to me," remarked Oslin, "He took me in and has taught me a lot over the last years."

1984 marked the beginning of another venture in his life, that of a wine consultant business that has made him known throughout the state. In addition, he started and maintained a lawn and landscape business that grew. Leaving Ingleside in 2010, Oslin worked for several wineries in the area before landing his present situation as winemaker for Hartwood Winery and Caret Cellars.

When asked about the Virginia wine industry, Oslin said things grew too fast, and now wineries and vineyards are starting to feel the effects. At the beginning of the Virginia boom, many exotic vines were planted. In addition, vineyards planted vinefera vines that were not suited for the locations.

"Virginia needs to take a hard look at the vines they are growing and go back to the key varietals that do well in the state. There were too many crazy expectations by growers," he commented.

Today, Oslin has become one of the top consultants in Virginia, and has spawned many vineyards and wineries in the eastern section, including Loch Haven Vineyards, Caret Cellars in Caret, and The Forge in Kilmarnock.

His expertise has played a large part in the Virginia wine industry's movement ahead of many other parts of the country in a systematic and steady course.

THE LOSS
Summer 2013

*...But seek ye first the kingdom of God and His righteousness,
and all these things shall be added unto you.* (Matthew 6.33)

After ten days of stuck fermentation on two carboys of
Traminette must I was making wine from, I finally got the
correct yeast to break the cycle that would not allow
fermentation to commence. I mixed the yeast with warm water
and some sugar, then added it to the must. I picked up one
carboy to shake it and after it was shaken, when putting it down,
it slipped and hit the other carboy, shattering both.

I stood and said,"I cannot believe I just did that."

Although this batch of wine has been a complete
frustration to me, I was looking forward to it more than I
realized. When the carboys broke, it was as if three years of
work was soaking into the ground.

Since then, I have grieved, and why should I not grieve?
With the scenario going through my head, there was a part of me
that did not believe this happened, that I would awaken from a
deep sleep and discover all this was just a bad dream. This was a
loss, not just a misplaced item, but a real loss. It hurt, bad.

The reality is, however, the juice is gone. There is always
next year, but the juice from the Traminette harvest this year is
gone, soaking in the ground. Dreams of a wine to send to
Indianapolis this summer are dashed. Envisioned Christmas
presents are watering the grass.

Every part of my being feels super sensitized since this
happened. I had no idea how much I had invested until it was
gone. I hope I can take this concentrated sense and apply it to
other parts of my life.

Spiritually, I have seen myself growing, but with plenty of room for more growth. If I can put all this energy into an "added thing" [in reference to Matthew 6:33], then it is my prayer that I will in turn recognize the possibility that lies within me as I make a similar investment into the Kingdom of God.

Intellectually, this has been a learning experience for both Diane and me. We have said that each year in the vineyard gives us a different perspective as to the care needed and how to implement such care. This year, in addition to caring for the vines, we get to have a harvest of the fruits of our labor for the first time , and watch as the juice is extracted from said fruit. So we learn...

I have learned and I have mourned my mistakes. Hopefully next time, I will do things in such a way that safety, and the preservation of previous labor, is insured.

In time, the pain will not be as sharp and other things will come to take the place of this incident. I guess it's time to move on.

So, this is to say goodbye to what I think would have been a wonderful wine, it would have been fun, it would have been good, but the truth is, it will not be.

LOCH HAVEN VINEYARDS: SPRING 2015

I have been spending a lot of time in my vineyard lately, it is that time of year. The buds have burst and the green new growth is breath taking. Of course I should say that or I would not be in this business. After all, there is not much money in it on the scale I work.

There is, however, something that calms the soul when working the vines. My wife, Diane and I will often go out to the vineyard with the idea of staying only fifteen minutes and come back an hour and a half later. Besides the fact there is always something to do, it is a peaceful place in which something is always going on.

We live in Sparta. For those who do not know where that is, it is south east of Bowling Green. Bowling Green, Fredericksburg and Ashland are all suburbs of Sparta. Our road is very busy for that part of the county.

We are constantly asked by our friends who drive by, "What were you doing in your vineyard the other day?" It is how they identify me.

This year the vineyard has surprised us. We have had two hard winters in a row. In between the two winters, last year we had two days of frost in April just as the buds were about to open up. As a result of the frost and a killer hail storm in June, we lost almost all of our crop plus a large number of vines. Most of our friends who drive by on Sparta Road happen to be farmers and when they found what occurred in our vineyard, they just shook their heads and bid me welcome to the world of agriculture.

But getting back to this year, I had written off a number of my Sangiovese vines, describing it to one friend as a "ghost town" due to the fact that everything appeared to be dead and I would not be receiving any crop this year or several years to come. Much to my delight, as I was cleaning up the vineyard for this season, I noticed a number of what looked like grape vines. In fact, they were grape vines.

Although they will not bear for several years, the comeback amazed me. Not all revived, but I was very thankful for those vines that did. It gave me hope for the future. On the other side of the vineyard, the Traminette vines are beautiful. Diane mentioned she has never seen them look so good. A year ago, I agonized as hail completely denuded the vines, making me wonder if they would even survive the winter with a lot of the leaves gone. Through photosynthesis in the leaves, carbohydrates are stored and converted to sugars which provide food to last through the dormancy of winter. Some leaves grew back, but not as many as I had hoped for. To see them now after what they were put through is a wonderment to me.

Last year we were able to harvest less than one hundred pounds of grapes, as opposed to the four and one half tons we expected. But when weather shows its ugly side, things do not always happen the way we want. My main worry was not for the grapes as much as for the vines, which is supported by the idea that many winemakers hold dear, *wine is made in the vineyard, not in the winery.*

As much as I like and enjoy wine, the vineyard for me does something wine never will. Working in the vineyard draws on the very innermost part of my being and speaks loudly to the rest of me. Tending and watching vines grow, even when the worst happens, has shown me a completely different side of life, something man cannot replicate. It makes a creationist out of me.

Enjoy a glass of wine and remember where it came from and what the vines may have gone through.

CARET CELLARS
Spring, 2015

The Middle Neck Peninsula is home to one of the newest and most important additions to the wine industry in Eastern Virginia. RD Thompson and his wife, Junghee, bought a piece of land off of Route 17 in Caret Virginia in 2006. The land that Thompson bought was at one time part of the Carneal Plantation, but was subdivided and sold. Grapes were planted at the vineyard by Thompson in 2007, and is soon to become Caret Cellars, one of the newest additions to the growing list of wineries in Virginia.

Agriculture is not new to Thompson, who hails from Walla Walla, Washington. He stated that in his family it was a rite of passage when a young man turned fourteen to go work on the family farm during the summer or when ever they were needed. Farm life turned out not to be his pursuit however, as he served in the United States Air Force for twenty five years after studying chemistry in college.

Again, contrary to his background, Thompson was not a chemist for the government, but was an Air Force Chinese linguist in Korea for twelve years where he also studied and became a Korean linguist. It was in Korea that he met his wife, Junghee. After retiring from the military and working for a government contractor at Quantico Marine Corps Base for twenty years, Thompson decided it was time for a lifestyle change. Starting a vineyard in Caret won out over owning a cattle ranch in Texas, which proved to be a good choice for them as well as for wine lovers in Virginia.

Many who have decided to make their mark with Virginia wine have found this can be a cruel business. In 2009, Thompson harvested a small but encouraging crop. In 2010, the entire crop was lost to a virus. While the vines were not lost, the fruit was rendered useless. Since then, Thompson has learned the necessity of preventative maintenance required in the vineyards of the Old Dominion, and the vast differences between vines from eastern and those from the western and northwestern part of the country. Bill Swain, former wine maker at Ingleside Vineyards, once commented that when he first started working in vineyards in California, he sprayed because he felt like he should. Coming to Virginia, he sprayed because he had to.

Thompson commented, "I have set up a spray schedule, and if it is time to spray, I spray, no matter what. I have learned that's what it takes."

As with many who come into this industry fresh, mistakes teach more than anything. Thompson's spraying paid off, with 2014 being a banner year as he was able to harvest seven tons of Sangiovese, four tons of Merlot and four tons of Chardonnay from less than five acres of vines. Rogers Ford Winery was the recipient of most of these grapes, but Thompson stated he has held on to a large number of them to make his own wine.

Thompson has built the vineyard and is now in the process of building a winery bit by bit. Not one who has a multi-million dollar line of credit, he has bought equipment as he has found it available, here a piece, there a piece, always with a watchful eye on the financial balance. At present, the wine production building has been completed.

Floyd Oslin of NuVines Vineyard Consultant and Management Services, a vineyard and winemaking guru in much of Virginia and southern Maryland, has been instrumental in developing this project. As winemaker for Thompson, he has been able to make enough wine to give Caret Cellars a good beginning supply when they officially start up.

Thompson has five and a quarter acres of grapes planted, but hopes to add five more acres in the near future with the vision of producing two thousand cases of wine per year. In production are a number of wines including Sangiovese, Rosatto, and White Merlot.

The Sangiovese, which Thompson states is his favorite, is full bodied with excellent tannins giving its black cherry taste a very rich and drinkable sensation. The French oak tasting adds a smokey flavor that is memorable and would pare well with a piece of red meat or pork.

The Rosatto is a wine that can be enjoyed on the back deck with dark chocolate. The grapes were so full of juice that after harvesting and going through the crush-destemming process, it was not necessary to press them. This wine is what is known as a free run wine. With a nose of red raspberry, the taste is the same but a bit off dry, giving a refreshingly elegant experience. The oaking on this wine supports the taste of the raspberry and accentuates its demeanor.

The White Merlot is, without a doubt, the queen of the winery. The wine is ninety percent Merlot, pressed immediately so none of the color of the skins remains in the wine. An additional five percent of Chardonel from Haymount Vineyards in Caroline County and five percent Vignioner from Thompson's own vines is added. A perfect match for either a poultry or seafood dinner, providing a richness and lush finish elevating the entire meal.

In general, there are a lot of big, heavy wines being produced now, both oaked and unoaked that have a tendency to bully their taste, taking over whatever they are served with. The wines of Caret Cellars are going to show the market that Virginia can produce a quality wine that is well structured and flavorful, without having to be a big muscle wine, joining those wine producers who already share a similar vision.

Caret Cellars has arrived! Opening in August of 2015, people have visited the tasting room to find ground breaking wines that are setting a new standard for blending in Virginia.

HARTWOOD WINERY
October, 2015

The wine industry in Virginia has exploded in recent years with the number of vineyards and wineries increasing. It has been said the Old Dominion wine producers are in an experimental stage as new varieties of grapes are coming into the state, adding to what is already here, and in some cases, replacing those that have not done well. The most rare asset to this burgeoning industry are mentors. Not just those with degrees in viticulture and oenology, but those who have been around for a while and are willing to take in the new people starting out.

In Stafford County, Jim Livingston is such a mentor, having been a father to many who have had the idea of being vintners. The success of Livingston's Hartwood Winery speaks of the work he has put into what he loves, and is a place of learning for the people who have taken the time to listen and work with him, gleaning from the years of experience he possesses.

Growing up in Carter County, Tennessee, Livingston's mother was a master cook and herbologist who gathered plants from the surrounding forest. At the dinner table, there was always moonshine to drink, which at that time was legal if used for personal consumption.

"I believe my talent at wine making came from my mother," stated he said, "She used to make the moonshine, also."

Educated as a librarian at East Tennessee, Livingston started making wine in college. To accommodate childhood polio, he was given a dorm room with a tub, in which he made a wine that he provided for faculty and administration. Several events involving high level administrators featured his bathtub wine. His education in wine was not in a classroom, however.

Livingston's mentor was the winemaker at Ingleside, Dr. Jacques Recht, who graduated from Bordeaux University and was the final protege of the famed oenologist Emile Peynaud. Dr. Recht noted Livingston's talent for working with wine, and took him under wing.

"Jacques used to work us hard, " he commented, "Not just in the field, but in the lab as well, teaching us to blend wines."

In addition to studying under Dr. Recht, Livingston traveled from Prince William County where he worked in the public schools as a librarian, to Burnley Vineyards in Barboursville, Virginia, learning to do everything that needed to be done in a winery. Jim Law at the time was offering courses on viticulture and oenology, and of course, Livingston was there.

With the help and advice of Lucy Morton, Hartwood Winery was started as a commercial winery in 1981 and then as a farm winery in 1989. Now one of the landmarks in the Fredericksburg region, Hartwood Winery participates in the Grapes and Grains Trail which includes tours of four wineries, three breweries and a distillery, spread throughout Stafford and Spotsylvania counties and the City of Fredericksburg.

Livingston stated that the wine industry in Virginia is changing with the larger wineries starting up and turning vineyards into wedding chapels and event centers to support themselves. The smaller wineries make a quality wine but are often overshadowed by the larger ones with their concerts and other happenings. To date, Hartwood Winery is active in assisting smaller wineries get past the learning curve involved in startup, offering advice and giving hands on experience.

Jim Livingston has been a part of the wine industry in Virginia for almost forty years and has seen a lot of changes. There are some constants: his expertise and love of wine, and his heart towards those who want to learn.

Hartwood Winery wines reflect Livingston's life's work.

Two of them that should be tasted when visiting:

Hartwood Station White - A blend of Chardonel and Rkatsitelli. The Chardonel adds a hint of apples, pears and perfuming. Rkatsitelli, a wine made from a grape originating in the Georgian Republic of Russia, gives a spiciness that enhances the wine experience. This wine pairs well with fish, fowl, or pork and is also delightful by itself.

The 2012 Tannat - This deep red French varietal offers a beautiful complexity and balanced tannins resulting from twenty four months of aging in oak barrels. This is a good wine to age.

BOTTLE CRAZY

August, 2015

Lately it has been a busy time for the Virginia's wine industry. Many do not think about what goes into their favorite bottle of wine until they begin to be aware of grapes being picked in the latter part of August. The truth is, in addition to the care of the vines that has continued all summer, the crunch time starts well ahead of harvest.

In order to make room for the juices after they are crushed from the harvested grapes, the wine in the barrels and tanks needs to be bottled. This process starts at the very last of July and continues through the middle of August, usually finishing up just before the ripe grapes are brought in.

While many of the larger wineries have automated pieces of equipment that take care of bottling, corking and labeling with one operation, most of the smaller farm wineries located throughout the state have to deal with bottling on a different scale with machinery that is not as technically advanced. No matter what size the operation, equipment must be sanitized. The wine is usually pumped from a holding tank to an elevated one. From the elevated tank the wine is fed by gravity into a bottle filler.

A common bottling operation involves one person emptying cases of bottles on a table. The individual working the four to six bottle filler takes the bottles and inserts the fill tubes into the bottles. They have to watch to see that the bottle is filled with wine to the proper level and take it off, putting an empty bottle in its place. Another individual adds either CO_2 or Nitrogen gas to keep air out which will oxidize and spoil the wine.

On to the corker, who, in most cases, uses a hand corker that leaves the individual working it with aching hands by the end of the session. For those fortunate enough, an automatic corker can be used in which the corks are poured into a hopper and automatically fed into position so that once a button is pushed, the filled and gassed bottle of wine has a cork inserted into the bottle correctly. For the home wine maker, whether using a store-bought kit or a limited amount of grapes to make wine, the corker may be a scissor shaped device with the cork placed in position and then the mouth of the corker put over the mouth of the bottle. When the handles are pulled down (hopefully keeping the corker straight as this is done), the cork goes into the bottle. Often this leaves a dimple in the end of the cork, and if not done properly, the cork will not go the whole way into the bottle.

In the winery, after the cork is inserted, there is a process of wiping off the bottles, usually done by an individual with a damp rag. The bottles are then placed back in the cases they came from and stacked on a pallet. Hopefully, there is a pallet jack or fork lift around to move the pallet of cases to a storage area.

Depending on the amount of wine to be bottled and the number of people available to man the various stations, the time it takes to bottle the wine varies. Interestingly enough, workers get into a rhythm and can move rather rapidly. Recently, four of us bottled seventy six cases (twelve bottles to a case) of wine using a four bottle filler and a non automatic corker. Another time six of us, using an automatic corker, bottled eighty cases, but it did not seem to go any faster. Immediately upon finishing the bottling of the last of the wine, it is time to begin picking the grapes.

Drink what you like, but remember where it came from and what went into the wine you are drinking.

THE U-BOAT
October, 2015

In a winery, when bottling is finished late summer, harvest is staring vintners square in the face almost immediately. For even the smallest vineyard, this is a time of calculated waiting, with the hope the birds and deer do not get to the grapes before it reaches the winemaker's criteria for ripeness.

The ripeness of the grape is often a point of contention between the viticulturist, who wants to get his fruit harvested before wildlife uses the vineyard as a banquet table, and the winemaker who wants the clusters to hang as long as possible in order to achieve the desired sugar content (brix), balanced with the acidity (Ph) in order to make a more perfect wine. The abuse of the vines by animal life is often blamed on the winemaker who, according to the viticulturist, procrastinated getting the harvest done.

Despite whoever wins out in this contentious battle, the grapes are picked, usually with the help of an army of volunteers or hired labor. Grapes are collected in containers called lugs, which hold approximately twenty five to thirty pounds. Full lugs are collected, and then transported to the crush pad.

The crush pad is a concrete pad where the most intense activity in processing the grapes occurs. It is here that the full lugs are weighed and then emptied into the crusher-destemmer. This machine not only separates the grapes from the stems and discharges them, it also breaks the skins of the grapes for the next step in the process. The famous television episode involving Lucille Ball in a large vat filled with grapes showed a process in which both crushing and pressing were accomplished by manpower, or in this case, comedic power.

When making red wine, the crushed and de-stemmed grapes are pumped to a container where yeast is added and fermentation takes place. Potassium metabisulfate is added to kill any natural air born yeasts. Fermentation usually takes about ten days or more for most wines. After fermentation, reds are returned to the crush pad and put in the press. In the process of producing a rose or a rosatto, the grapes are pressed after one or two days, due to the fact that the color in a wine comes from the skins, which along with seeds, contributes to the tannin in the wine. In a normal situation, after fermentation the grapes are pressed, but caution is used so as not to press them too much. Over pressing is another source of tannin as the skins and seeds are pressed against the sides of the press and release the tannins they carry. As opposed to red wine grapes, white wine grapes are pressed immediately at harvest. Both red and white grapes are pumped from the press to a holding tank where fermentation can commence, or continue to ferment as in the case of some reds.

The most interesting part of this process is the press itself. As one can imagine, there are many different types and sizes of presses, from ones designed for home use that press only a couple of hundred pounds at a time to extremely large electronic ones that tout the age of technology. For those who are true blue to this industry, it is difficult to beat the more mechanical bladder presses. At Hartwood Cellars, Jim Livingston uses what is called a "U-Boat"because of its long round shape. Those who operate this press are known as *U-Boat Captains.* The crushed and de-stemmed grapes are pumped from the crusher de-stemmer to the press through a flexible three inch hose which is held in place by the *Torpedo Loader.*

When the press is full, it is closed and a bladder in the middle is inflated with air pressing against the grapes inside and causing the juice to flow out through small holes in a screen. After pressing, the skins left inside the press are like dry cakes that need to be peeled off the sides. Often, when loading a press, juice will begin to flow prior to pressing. This is known as free flowing juice, and where the wineries are big enough to accumulate a lot of free flowing juice, for some wines, it is all that is used to make some wines.

From field to fermentation this labor intensive process offers a fascinating look at one aspect of making wine.

CAROLINE VINES
August, 2013

Virginia, in recent years, has been referred to as the Napa Valley of the East producing wines that are achieving international acclaim as the science of raising wine grapes (viticulture) is maturing and knowledge consistently grows with experience.

In February 2012, Virginia Governor McDonnell's office released The Economic Impact of Wine and Grapes on the State of Virginia by Frank, Rimmerman + Co. LLP, commissioned by the Virginia Wine Board. As of the release date, Virginia was ranked number five in the nation with over 200 wineries. It was reported that the Virginia wine industry provided the Commonwealth $747,092,00 in revenue and wages.

As of the end of 2012, 7,532 tons of wine grapes were produced in Virginia which sold for an average of $1669.00 per ton. Of the total tonnage produced, 5,603 tons were of the European, or Vinefera variety and sold at an average of $1817.00 per ton.

At the 2013 winter technical meeting of the Virginia Vineyards Association, Virginia Secretary of Agriculture indicated more grapes need to be planted to keep up with the increased growth of Virginia wine sales. It was reported that Virginia has shown an eight percent increase in wine sales but the acreage of vineyards has not grown significantly enough to support growth. Approximately 3000 acres were being used at the time for vineyards.

When I first started talking about growing wine grapes, I was told by local vineyard owners that it was an awful lot of work, something I learned oh too well. A season in the vineyard begins in February and runs into October, depending on the variety of grapes grown.

After pruning in February, I find spraying one of the most time consuming parts of the work in the vineyard. Sprays are used for protection of the vines for everything from various mildews from the early spring rains to infestations of Japanese beetles and cut worms.

In addition to spraying, there is the constant training of vines as they grow. Often I have left my vineyard pleased with the work done, only to find in a couple of days the vines have grown and retraining must occur. In addition to training, the lower branches of the vines must be removed so as not to rob the fruit of nutrients that come up through the main branch. This "suckering" of the vine changes the entire appearance of the vineyard.

Often, as grapes grow, the leaves that shade them, known as the canopy, must be thinned so as not to block sunlight and air and to prevent mildew to take its toll on the fruit.

The major factor that must be contended with in the vineyard is concern for the vines. Cheryl Kellert of Gray Ghost Winery and Vineyards so aptly puts it,"We operate on a state of fear for what may happen to the vines."

Loch Haven Vineyards started out as a dream of a few rows of grapes in our back yard in Bowling Green with which to play and has turned into an almost full time job. My wife, Diane and I, three years ago planted five hundred vines on some land in Sparta, purchased in 2010. We planted two varieties, Sangiovese and Traminette.

In our third season, we are at present working to train the vines into what will be the most advantageous form for the production of fruit. This year we expect to produce about one thousand pounds of grapes. Because this is not a large enough quantity to sell, this fall we will make wine and keep it for our own consumption and for gifts to friends.

While there will always be fruit retained for personal wine making, the main purpose of Loch Haven Vineyards is to produce a quality grape for sale to the surrounding wineries.

In northern Caroline County, located near Rappahannock Academy, lies Haymount, home of George and Linda Fisher, and four acres of grape vines that make up Haymount Vineyards. Planted in 2005, Haymount has what viticulturist Floyd Oslin calls "textbook vines", because of the meticulous care given to them by George Fisher. When asked about the care of his vines, Fisher stated that "a good nutrient program is key to growing vines."

It should be noted that in addition to healthy vines, the vineyard itself is extremely well kept, with vines that grow in the midst of grass manicured between rows of vines.

"I used to have people come in and work the vines, but each year I became more and more dissatisfied with what they did,"remarked Fisher,"So now I take care of them myself. It's a full time job. My wife knows where to find me, in the vineyard."

In 2012, Fisher harvested petite verdot, chardonel, merlot, cabernet sauvignon and syrah grapes and made wine in a building on the estate that is known as the "Bunga Bunga House." There the grapes are hand crushed for fermentation and then the juices are squeezed into carboys where the real wine process is carried out.

Concerning his wines, Fisher commented, "I having been working on the whites for some time, this year I will be working on perfecting the reds."

In the eastern side of Caroline, just off of Mattaponi Trail on Fork Bridge Road, lies the Upshaw home place. Originally 4000 acres just after the Revolutionary War, over the generations, it has been divided among surviving relatives until now each of the five remaining Upshaw brothers each own 50 acres.

Bill Upshaw describes the soil as a loamy sand that turns into red clay about one foot down. The vines that were planted have grown under the care of Bill and his brother Ed, who inherited the piece of land where the vines are located. Much of the land, other than that where a house now stands, lies in quail preserve. Ed stated he grows certain grasses and leaves them alone so that quail have a place to roost. With wildlife cameras around the yard, Ed stated he sees everything from bobcats to quail.

Bill, who at present lives in Fredericksburg, planted about 15 Muscadine vines eight years ago of three different varieties: Sugargate, Ison and Couart. Also grown on the property are some Concord. Bill described the Muscadine grape as disease and blight resistant with very little maintenance required other than pruning the vines at the end of the winter in preparation for spring growth. Many other varieties at this time of year with the amount of rain that has fallen show some signs of mildew and black rot, but these vines were spotless, strong and extremely healthy.

At one time the grapes, which according to Bill get as big around as a half dollar coin, were used to make a sweet wine. The harvest is plentiful enough to make wine for lots of Christmas gifts and to just give away to friends. At present, although some wine from previous crops remain, the grapes are used for jellies and juices.

Ed stated,"These are for my grandchildren when they come to visit, so they can have something to eat while they play."

Vineyards can vary in size from the backyard trellis area to the vineyards in Northern and Western Virginia that cover many acres. As if an answer to the dream of the original colonists, wine is truly becoming a money crop in Virginia.

LAKE ANNA WINERY
September, 2012

Most of the wineries in Virginia have the designation of "Farm Wineries", in which the majority of the grapes used to produce wine come from the actual location. If one were to look closer, however, they would see that a lot of the farm wineries are also family wineries which could be defined as establishments where not only is the business passed down the line from one generation to the next, but more importantly, the entire family is involved working at various tasks.

Jeff and Eric Heidig, are the second generation to work the vines at Lake Anna Winery. The origins of the winery began on a business trip to France by founder Bill Heidig. Already in possession of the land where the winery is presently located, he inquired of some of his associates what would be good to plant there. Not surprisingly, they responded that grapes would be the optimum crop to grow.

In 1983, Bill and his wife Ann planted their first vines. With 2000 seyval, 250 cabernet sauvignon, and 1000 chardonnay vines planted, they learned first hand what was involved in starting a vineyard. In 1987, after selling grapes to local wineries, the Heidigs made their first wine in their basement. In 1989, the first vintage of Seyval Blanc was bottled and sold and soon after, Lake Anna Winery became a reality at festivals around Virginia.

Not wanting to be just another winery, Jeff and Eric have utilized the culture of the area, specifically the battles of the Civil War which took place nearby, to set their wines apart. Their Spotsylvania Claret has a variety of different labels depicting different battles with many of the patrons of the winery having collected the entire set.

Because it is in the Piedmont section of Virginia, it is not surprising that clay makes up the majority of the soil here. Combined with the lake climate from nearby Lake Anna, the second largest lake in the state, the terroir has proven to be advantageous in the production of wine grapes.

At present, the twenty one acres planted produce approximately sixty tons of grapes annually which represents seventy five percent of the grapes needed for the winery with the remainder of the tonnage bought throughout the state. The winery itself produces from 5000 to 5500 cases of wine annually with plans to expand eventually to 8000 cases with10000 cases being the maximum they would want to handle.

Of the dozen or so wines produced, probably the best known is the Enigme an award winning wine with a gold medal at the Virginia State Fair, made up of three varietals of grapes, tanat, chambercin and merlot. While this wine has a big, bold taste, it is anything but heavy. A number of lovely flavors come out making this a complex and delightful pairing for meals in which a number of flavors prevail.

For the white wine lovers, the 2010 Chardonnay Barrel Select, made in the European tradition is a must to try. One hundred percent Chardonnay, aged in oak for ten months, this wine offers a taste not found in Virginia anywhere else. The taste of English toffee and caramel is not something put in the description for marketing purposes, the taste is really there. That, matched with a hint of tropical fruit makes this a wine that is beautiful with a lingering finish, preceded by a unique palate of consistent elegance. Upon tasting, the immediate thought that came to mind was of hot chicken soup on a cold day. This is a wine that warms the soul.

The Bellehaven Cabernet Franc, made in 2008, is one hundred percent cabernet franc, which is one of Virginia's signature grapes, and exhibits a deep, rich color that belies a wine filled with the flavors of mocha and ripe berries. As if that was not enough, the full finish that wraps up the entire experience is laced with hazelnuts, giving it the distinction of being one of the better Virginia cabernet francs tasted.

The Spotsylvania Claret not only shows scenes of battles around the area on its labels, it also shows a bright, lively flavor of red cherries, red raspberry, and herbs in a delightful medium bodied experience that is sure to please even the most stringent of palates. Made up of merlot, cab franc and chardonnay with a touch of residual sugar, gives this wine the taste structure and character that allows it to be enjoyed with a variety of different foods.

The wines of Lake Anna Winery are most impressive and make for a stop that must not be missed. Closed only on Thanksgiving, Christmas and New Years, and opened from 11:00 AM-5:00 PM everyday except Sunday, 1:00 PM-5:00 PM, one finds there a welcoming and knowledgeable staff that enhance the visit.

THINGS

THE FIRST KISS
August, 2012

Most everyone remembers their first kiss. In a closet playing teenage games or sneaking one in while dropping off a date, it is inevitable. What about the first kiss with the one who will be your soul mate, blowing us into another dimension? The one sending sparks flying and angels singing and all of sudden brightening all the colors of the world. Do you remember the first kiss?

Did something happen, or did somebody say something making the kiss so memorable? For many, it is never forgotten and that is a good thing. I will never forget the first time I kissed my wife. Prior to marriage, our initial friendship lasted for a year and a half, we dated for another year and a half, and our engagement lasted for a year. We finally married in 1978.

The monumental night when our lips first met, I was walking Diane across the college campus to her dorm. We walked by the end of the building and I noticed the way the light shown, we walked where the shadows fell. We were in darkness.

I stopped. I kissed her. I can still see the gleam in her eyes.

She looked up at me and said, "You're nice."

Because I had trouble hearing, I thought she said,"Good night," so I left.

THE SMITHFIELD HOG STORY
September, 2014

One of my many jobs involved searching out small community stores in which to sell the food product my company produced. Quite often this would lead down some country road I would not travel otherwise. The sights to be seen usually provided interest, specific to the area in which I found myself.

For instance, Smithfield, Virginia. Everyone knows this area is famous for its hog production and the Smithfield meat processing plant.   In this area, every house kept two pens on their property, one for the hogs they raise to sell on the market and the other for the dogs they use to hunt.   Sometimes a third sight existed, not to be ignored: the pet hog in the front yard.

The pet hog is kept in a smaller sty or tied to a stake with a shelter similar to where you might find a dog is confined in a neighborhood. This pet is not canine, definitely porcine. With this in mind, please believe me when I tell you at first I was not surprised when one day while working in this area, I saw at a distance what turned out to be one of the strangest sights I have ever seen.

I glanced up the road and detected at a distance a man walking with a cane, leading what appeared to be a large dog attached to a leash. Mind you, there is nothing odd about such a sight, except for the gait with which they both walked. The man had a limp that was apparent every other step and the large dog like animal had a limp resulting from what appeared to be a game hind leg. My curiosity got the better of me so I went to check out this odd pair.

As I drove my car up to them, I realized the dog like animal was, in fact, a hog on a leash. This was no big deal as this was probably the man's pet hog. What shocked my senses was the hog's wooden prostheses attached where his right hind leg was normally.   The prostheses went all the way up to the hip and attached with leather straps around the hog's torso.

I drove up to this interesting sight, rolled down my window and said, "That is some hog you have there, sir."

"Yep," was his only reply.

At this point, I heard myself burst out with one of the most inane comments I have ever made in my life,"Excuse me, mister, but your hog's got a wooden leg!"

Again, came the man's singular comment "Yep."

"Well, that's some hog."

The man leaned against my car and said, "He sure is. Now how about you climb outen your car and I'll tell you jest how special he is."

Again my curiosity got the better of me. Being on a narrow, back country road, I did not think if I stopped, I would be causing much of a traffic problem, so I turned off the ignition and stepped out of the car bracing myself for a long saga about this hog, which it was.

"Fust of all, le' me tell you this here hog saved my life and my missus' life, too," the man stated with obvious pride, "This here is one damn special hog."

"He's al'ays been a pet, in his sty in the front yard, so one night me and the missus went to bed just like always. Well, somehow that night, a fire broke out in our house and this hog busted outen his sty, ran up the poach steps, busted in the house, up the staiahs to the second story and woke us up in our bedroom so's we could get outen the house jest in the nick o' time. Yep, thaiah is one damn special hog."

"Well, did he hurt his leg while saving you and your wife?"

"No, why would you think sech a thaing?" came his quizzical reply.

For the second time in such a short while I made the infamous comment, "Mister, your hog's got a wooden leg!"

The man gave me a look of sullen disappointment, and shaking his head said,"Damn boy, don't you know nothin'? You got a hog special like this un, you don't eat him all at once!"

THE WAIT

June, 2013

How long would he have to watch? Boredom crept into his young soul and as a breeze began to blow, giving some relief to the scorching sun, his thoughts began to wander, his head began to nod.

A rude awakening greeted him as something slimy slid up and down on his face. Drool and the rough skin against his cheek immediately brought him back to the reality from which he had tried to escape. The first thing he noticed was his hands were empty, yet nothing had changed. Still there, red and white, laughing at him, telling him that although this seemed to be really boring, this was not going to change.

Upset with himself for losing concentration, he fixed his gaze anew, determined to be ready when the time came, if it ever would. This is how he spent most of the afternoon, determined to keep his watch, yet finding himself distracted. Fighting the ever present desire for his mind to wander, brought about by the tedium of waiting versus the conviction that he needed to keep his attention sharp, he sat.

When the moment finally came, he was surprised not at the sight, but at the feeling. He noticed the initial movement of what he had so long fixed his eyes upon and then it went under only to pop up again and then went under a second time hard and fast. Energy seemed to go into his arms.

He could feel the movement as it went back and forth in a frantic effort to go deeper and farther away. He sensed its quest for survival as it was pulled upward. He worked as he had been taught as it valiantly fought a losing battle, reaching the edge with a mighty last ditch surge in order to break free. Up, up into the air with a display that brought forth from him a sound of awe as he observed with almost unbelieving eyes. As the dog barked, he shrieked with delight for all to hear and exclaimed,"Dad! Look! I caught a fish!"

MULTIPLE MYELOMA SEMINAR

September, 2014

On Saturday, September 20, 2014, Mike Alsop and Harolynn Quash held a seminar at Second Mt. Zion Baptist Church in Dawn, Virginia to give participants an awareness of the disease known as Multiple Myeloma. The main speaker was Dr. John McCarty, Director of the Bone Marrow Transplant Unit of the Massey Cancer Center at Virginia Commonwealth University-Medical College of Virginia. McCarty is one of three specialist on a team including Drs. Harold Chung and Amir Tool.

According to Alsop, it is sometimes referred to as a blood cancer in the bone marrow, where the bone marrow is affected causing high protein levels in the blood which affects the kidneys. The most common symptom is its attack on the immune system due to the accumulation of irregular platelets in the bone marrow. In addition, the effect on ones skeletal system is that it causes pin holes in the bones.

Both Alsop and Quash stood up and gave their account of their fight with Multiple Myeloma. It was stated several times this condition masks itself in various ways. Quash was being treated for rheumatoid arthritis, and though she did have some arthritis, the main problem was this rare form of cancer. Alsop stated that in addition to the fatigue and lack of energy that everyone feels, there was a calcium buildup in his rib cage and severe back pain.

It was stated the first bone marrow transplant is done harvesting their own bone marrow and then using bone marrow from a close match to their own, usually a relative. Both Alsop and Quash had siblings who matched. Alsop mentioned and was echoed by Quash that this was a very difficult time, but their faith was what kept them going.

Dr. McCarty, described by Alsop as a doctor who can

break down the most complex medical procedures into simple layman's terms, spoke describing the procedure a patient goes through in receiving a bone marrow transplant. Years ago, according to McCarty, the procedure included actually going into the bone marrow of the individual and doing a manual harvest.

Today, through a multiple step procedure, the process is much easier. The donor gives themselves a series of shots causing an apheresis, or movement of the marrow into the blood stream. The blood is then processed and the marrow is removed and cleaned up. For the recipient, they are given a dose of chemotherapy to rid their system of the myeloma cells. Liquids are given to flush the body out prior to putting in the donated bone marrow. This procedure affects the immune system and patients have to wear a mask or stay at the hospital in an environment that is germ free.

As a result of new technology and increased bed space at the cancer center, more bone marrow transplants are able to take place. In 2000, approximately fifty transplants were done as opposed to two hundred in the past twelve months according to McCarty.

McCarty mentioned that in Caroline County alone, there are sixteen or seventeen cases reported of Multiple Myeloma. Alsop mentioned four cases that existed in Salem Baptist Church, a congregation of approximately two hundred fifty. Research has yet to detect any common denominator between cases. In Caroline, there is nothing adverse that appears to be causing the myeloma.

After a brief question and answer period, a light lunch was served and people were able to talk with the seminar participants more about their disease. A condition called Survivor Guilt was discussed by Alsop. Both he and Quash stated they have known people who have died from Multiple Myeloma, yet they are in remission. Both stated they believed God is in complete control of this situation and they feel it necessary to inform the public of this disease and the advancements in treating it along with their story of how they dealt with Multiple Myeloma.

ONE DAY IN A DOCTOR'S OFFICE RESTROOM
April, 2012

As I entered the restroom at the doctor's office, I noticed a gentleman I had seen in the waiting room. He appeared to be about six foot three inches tall and around one hundred eighty pounds. He was dressed casually in khakis, an oxford cloth shirt and was wearing those brown leather deck shoes that have leather cords running through them. With slightly graying hair he looked to be in his late forties or early fifties. The distinguishing characteristic that struck me was that he appeared as one who spoke little to anyone unless it was extremely necessary. I would not have paid any attention except for the fact that I was carrying a book of short stories which I laid on the counter next to the sink.

He took an inordinate amount of time looking at himself in the mirror after washing and drying his hands and as he left, I thought I heard him pick up something from the counter and walk out.

I arrived in the waiting room just in time to see him handing my book to an individual he was sitting across from and stating, "Here, try this one. It's pretty good."

Approaching him, I grabbed the book from his hand and said to him in a loud voice, "You have one heck of a nerve just taking someone's book."

"I thought it was part of a lend exchange program, so I just took it," he stammered in a surprised response as he rose from the chair to his full height. My reaction to this was simple, I hit him squarely in the face.

After I was done at the urinal, I washed and dried my hands, picked up my book, and left.

RODRIGUEZ'S JACKS

August, 2014

For all those who are involved in the wine industry, at least from a viticultural perspective, the idea that animals and insects find various parts of the vine much to their culinary delight is nothing new. There are as many precautions and devices that can be used as their are different predators. In Newtown, Virginia, Robert Rodriguez has found a unique approach to this dilemma, Jack Russell terriers.

The Jack Russell Terrier, a working dog, remains much the same as it was two hundred years ago, with an average height of ten to fifteen inches and weighing in at fourteen to eighteen pounds. Known for their aggressive nature, they were originally used for hunting small game such as foxes. Because they are fearless, they go down holes into the ground after animals. Occasionally, the Jack (as they are often called) is bred with fox terriers to keep them from over breeding.

Rodriguez has a vineyard of approximately ninety five vines and, because he lives off the beaten path with frontage on the Mattaponi River, he is open to all kinds of predators ranging from voles to ground hogs and raccoons who finds his varieties of grapes quite a delicacy.

"These dogs are very well mannered and like people," remarked Rodriguez,"but they hate animals and are not afraid of them."

He related how Firestorm Puff, one of his alpha dogs will actually attack and kill raccoons. The other alpha, Julia, goes after rabbits, but does it in a unique fashion. When she sees the rabbit, she will not attack it at first, but follows it, finding out where the warren is and then digs into the ground cleaning it out completely. Rodriguez commented that Puff and Julia, because of their dominant nature, cannot be let out of the kennel together, because each thinks that they are the main dog and will fight with the other. The two remaining dogs, Siri and Trump (who is related to the original Parson Terrier from England named Trump) work together or with the Puff or Julia.

Released from the kennel in the morning after all the neighbors have left for work, they have been known to kill predators who venture into their territory, even snakes. It is not uncommon to see them with their entire face buried in the ground, going after something. After killing the animals, they are deposited on the front porch, for the master's approval. Rodriguez mentioned that they are often taken to the vet for animal bites, particularly from raccoons. He said they learn how to handle snakes after the first confrontation, letting out a high pitched cry and relentlessly attacking them.

Recently, Rodriguez heard Trump and Julia getting very excited and went to investigate. To his surprise, they were going after a snapping turtle that measured twenty four to thirty inches in diameter. The snapper, with a head as large as the dog's head, paid little attention to their noise as it was in the process of laying eggs. To calm the dogs down, a small baby pool was put over the turtle so it could not be seen.

Loyal to master and family, Jacks are a fearless warrior, who in this case, are doing their best to enhance the Virginia Wine Industry.

MRS. MICKLEBERRY
February, 2012

When I was in high school I ran the mile and two mile during spring track. Not a very gifted athlete, my memories of these competitions was not breaking the tape at the finish line.

One of my best memories is that of Mrs. Betty Fairchilds yelling out as I passed in front of the grandstands, "Pick those knees up, Walter Scott! Stretch out your legs!"

I never thought I would ever meet anyone with her enthusiasm and love for sports until the winter of 2011-12 when I went to cover a Caroline High School basketball game and sat in front of Mrs. Mickleberry, as her son, Corey, who is the assistant basketball coach, worked. Her lively spirit and enjoyment of the game took me back years to the days of hearing Mrs. Fairchilds in the stands.

The fact that her son is the assistant coach is secondary. Mrs. Mickleberry not only loves the game, she knows it as well. She has one of those nice, pleasing voices that makes one enjoy talking with her yet at the same time can be heard above the sound of the Cavalier cheering squad encouraging the players and telling them what they should have done. What an asset to Cavalier basketball.

Talking with many of the athletes, I have heard many times they hate to play in front of half empty stands, the rush of hearing people cheer them on gives a lot of encouragement.

Thank you, Mrs. Mickleberry, for your voice at Caroline athletics. You would have loved watching basketball with Mrs. Fairchilds.

THE MODEL T
July, 2014

Since moving to Caroline County in 2004, I have enjoyed the scenic back roads that are in abundance. While traveling these roads, I have seen everything from woodlands to farms with tractors working in the fields planting and reaping various grains as well as beef cattle grazing. Perspective of that same scenery changes, however, from the front seat of a 1922 Ford Model T Touring car.

The Model T was the car made by Henry Ford from 1909 until 1927 so that everyday people could afford a car. Ford was not the first to have an assembly line, but he was the first to have one that moved and was also the first auto manufacturer to build a car with interchangeable parts. This was a nuts and bolts car that could be repaired by the least mechanically inclined individual. It should be noted that it was made when roads were not as they are today. Dirt roads, if there were any roads at all, were what this tough little car was made to ride. The Model T was referred to as buggy with a motor.

Ford, anxious to share his product, did not confine the sale of this classic to the United States. Each country had a different Model T according to the driving customs of that area. The American version was a three door vehicle that forced the driver to go through the passenger door, whereas in Canada they had four doors. The European models actually had the steering wheel and pedals on the opposite side to accommodate driving there.

Hollywood used Model T's, noticeably with Laurel and Hardy. What fan of these two can forget them getting a neck tie stuck in the hand windshield wiper during a down pour with the top blown back? In the movie Giant, James Dean can be seen working on one.

107

Wic Coleman Jr, the present owner and restorer of what is a classic vintage automobile, is the fourth generation in his family to own it. In 1923, his great grandfather, Douglas Heiter Coleman, bought the car for less than $400.00. It was then passed down to H.W. and Fred Coleman to Wic, Sr prior to Wic, Jr. inheriting it. He commented that the car was probably made in the winter of 1922 as it has a metal firewall, which was only used on cars made in the winter.

Due to the fact that Douglas Heiter Coleman was a forest warden, there was even rougher usage given this Tin Lizzie than just difficult road wear. Wic told of how it was used to go into the woods to fight forest fires. With the top down, fire fighters and their equipment would load up in the car and go to wherever the fire was located. On the wooden spoke wheels, it can be seen where a chain was wrapped around the spokes and then to a tree to act as a winch when the vehicle got stuck. At some point, the front axle was severely damaged, made obvious by the fact that the it had ball bearings instead of the standard cone bearing. The use of ball bearings was discontinued sometime around 1919. Wic, being the purist that he is, had the ball bearings replaced with the cone bearings used in the 1922 version.

Other than the ball bearings, top and seats (which were made by Southern Automotive especially for Wic), the car is made up of original equipment. Interesting to note, the frame is made up of wood that came from the packing crates that contained parts sent to Henry Ford's factory. The floor boards are made of tongue and groove boards from the same source.

Covering the frame is a body of very thin metal. With this particular Model T, the body was painted red, but has been restored to its original black. Henry Ford was reported to have made the comment that buyers can have any color they want as long as it is black.

Under the hood is a four cylinder, 177 cubic inch motor that boasts twenty horse power and tops out at 30-35 miles per hour. There are no filters, so it is necessary to check and change the oil frequently (Wic stated he changes the oil once a month). Also there are no pumps in the motor with the water turning to steam and circulating. As a result, of this configuration, it easy to throw a rod. The only meter on the dash is an amp meter for the six volt battery.   Starting off using the battery, once speed has built up, a switch is flipped and the magneto takes over, not only allowing faster speed, but a smoother ride as well.

Getting the motor started is done by a crank located on the front of the car, which in itself can be rather dangerous. Prior to cranking, the tractor like throttle has to be set just right or the crank can come back and cause serious injury to the person trying to start it.

"People would come to church with their arms in a sling from trying to get their Model T's started," commented Wic, "Especially in the winter. This is one temperamental vehicle."

Driving this car is not for the faint of heart. There are three pedals, none of which is for the gas., which uses a throttle. With the left most pedal depressed, the driver takes off and then releases it about half way to go in the lower speeds. Depressing the pedal all the way in puts the car in high gear. The second pedal was for reverse, and the third as a brake. Because the braking system is not like brakes in modern cars, the driver has to allow plenty of room to stop. The brake shoes, attached to the spoke wheel, are cast iron and pressed against each other to stop.

The tires (30x30 1/2 with fifty five pounds of air) have tubes and can be difficult to change for anyone except those who change them often. Putting some air in the tube helps and once on the wheel, there are grippers on the tires that fit into the wheel. Often used as a tractor, owners would put larger wheels on the back and convert the Tin Lizzie into the Doodle Bug. When the farming was done, the wheels could be changed back into the regular vehicle.

The most amazing thing about this vehicle is the ride.

With leaf springs underneath and coiled springs on the sides and seats that speak total comfort, the ride is smoother than can be expressed. Cruising through the back roads of Penola at a breezy 25 miles per hour on a beautiful spring day, I had to wonder why anyone would feel as if they need to go any faster.

Hats off to Wic Coleman, Jr. for restoring this wonderful piece of Americana.

A FAST ELECTRIC CAR
July, 2013

I have always been a closet admirer of the fast muscle cars that came out in the 60's and 70's. Though the body styles change, the speed and power of vehicles will always be something of a marvel to those of us in and outside of the speed closet.

We live in a world where everything is fast, from the cars we drive to the food we eat. Life is not slowing down at all, it is getting faster. In the midst of our speeding world comes the electric car. Here are some of the finest machines made by man in that they are energy efficient, and some are even fast.

It should be noted that what is deemed the fastest electric car is subject to change due to our ever changing technology and information. Consider when automobiles were first being developed, fifteen miles per hour was considered too fast and dangerous by many.

One of the fastest electric cars is the Rimac Automobili Concept One which was made in Croatia. In addition to being the most powerful electric car of its type when it was made, the propulsion system offers a design that sets it aside from other electric cars.

Thanks to an electric motor above each wheel, this vehicle has amazing handling and can reach speeds of up to 190 miles per hour. Accelerating from 0-62 MPH (100KPH) is achieved in 2.8 seconds as a result of a drivetrain with a capacity of up to 1088 HP and 3800Nm of torque.

This automobile contains an All Wheel Torque Vectoring System (AWTV) which is divided into a front and rear sub system with each having two symmetrical motor-controller-reduction-gearbox units.

These specific gearbox units allow each wheel to be

driven completely independent of the others. The power and torque transferred to the wheels can be adjusted up to one thousand times per second. There are Electronic Control Units that gather information for the systems from sensors all over the car.

Although the Concept One was revealed in 2011, it was not released on the market until 2013, and then with only a limited production of eighty eight vehicles. The sticker on this one ran a cool $980,000.00 with several preproduction models ordered by the Abu Dhabi Royals.

For years, companies have claimed to have the "car of the future," only to be superseded by the next sleek model that comes along. The technology behind the electric cars used to be the science of the future, but has now become the technology of the present, within the near future being further developments in this field.

Rimac has merely given us a glimpse of the mechanical and electric innovations we can expect. For now the Rimac Automobili Concept Car is the fastest car of the present that equipped solely with an electric system and delivers a high powered technical propensity. The question remains, what will the future hold? But seeing is believing. Check this out:

http://rimac.cro.net

http://www.youtube.com/watch?v=NaJUZIdDiFw

NAIL BITER BASEBALL: COURTLAND VS CAROLINE
April, 2013

Baseball is one of the more exciting spectator games I have had the privilege of covering. Those who have done even the minimal amount of study have found these contests to be packed with strategy and action. Players are constantly watching the position of opponents as well as signals from the coaches. Game situations are like a chess match when two teams get together and are aligned to the point that no one knows the outcome of the game until it has ended.

Take for instance, the rivalries in the Battlefield District High School. Courtland High School in Spotsylvania has long been an excellent competitor with Caroline High School. The excitement of the 2014 game built until the last inning. The point I make is best shown in this passage (which is one of my favorites in all of my sports writings):

The top of the seventh inning turned out to be a nail biter with Courtland scoring two runs to go up 3-2, but Caroline smelled comeback. In the bottom of the seventh, the last inning of regulation, Jonathan Didlake was walked and Ryan Hickman hit a double to put Didlake on third and himself on second. Another walk to Collin Hess loaded the bases and Rasharrd Harris came up to bat with two outs.

Harris played the pitcher to a full count, leaving a hard decision for the young man occupying the mound. If he throws a change up and misses, Harris walks, a run comes in and the pitcher has to face Jay Chapman and his heavy bat. The decision was for the fast ball which Harris nailed to right field, allowing two runners to score and the game to end with the score: Caroline 4, Courtland 3.

I SPENT THE MORNING WITH AN EAGLE
May, 2012

I spent the morning with an eagle.

Majestic, beautiful, he sat upon the top of a post in our vineyard in the rain. Occasionally he would raise his feathers as if to shake off the excess rain, but mostly he sat, looking this way and that, observing all that was around him, as if he were the guardian of the vineyard.

He was not particularly large, so I think he was probably a male, with a white head that was somewhat yellowed, giving the appearance of a young adult. His appearance was regal, as if he knew exactly who he was and why he was where he was. A sense of awe pervaded as I watched this magnificent creature.

The eyes were small and piercing, ever searching, ever seeing, ever knowing. They were portals to an active mind, intelligent and somewhat thoughtful as they perused the area around. The sharp beak, placed in the middle of this imposing face, spoke of the power this animal possessed. I had to wonder if he ever thought about all that he had, or, was he so gifted that he moved in it quite naturally without the conscious effort that we humans require?

His greatest gift to me this morning came at the very end of his visit. He flew. Majesty and grace unfurled as he circled our pond, beating his wings and soaring higher and higher, and then coming around again as if to give me one final look and a farewell until next time.

I spent the morning with an eagle.

IT IS ABOUT MIDNIGHT AND I AM NOT...
June, 2013

It is about midnight, and I am not wide awake, but I feel as if I can't go to sleep either. Something is bugging me, but I don't know what. Of course, no one else has that happen to themselves. Just me. This is reminiscent of when I was little and thought that I was the only one who could not see their face without looking in the mirror.

I think I am finding out what this blog stuff is all about. VENTING. It feels good to write, but there is still something bugging me. I took my meds tonight and it feels like they are stuck in my throat, which I know is crazy, but it happens. I just drank some water and ate a bunch of Oreo cookies, but it did not help. I think I am tired.

I had a big day today. I went to a meeting in Richmond put on by the Virginia Wine Board. We were discussing the future of the wine industry in Virginia. We broke up into small groups and brainstormed about different aspects of what is going on and what we should do about it. All day. I am tired.

I met some cool people and renewed some relationships, but the day was about working. Work, we did, all day. It was good because my attention was focused (no ADD attacks) as I sat and joined in the discussion about issues in the Virginia wine industry.

I really like wine and I like the wine industry in Virginia. It is a close knit group with everyone wanting the same thing: To promote Virginia wines.

I am really tired, enough of this. I'm going to bed.

VEGETABLES
March, 2009

When I was growing up I neither heard nor wanted to hear of vegans and vegetarians and now it is the latest rage. It should be noted that the days when I was little, cigarette commercials were still on television and smoking was considered the sophisticated thing to do. Maybe it is because I grew up in that era, I have to wonder about the children I see on television commercials today who are hungrily gobbling up vegetables.

Again, those were different days than the ones we live in now. Those were the days of the casseroles with canned vegetables that had that residual taste of the can from which they came. Could you imagine a cooking show today trying to grill canned asparagus? What went into the can were the parts that TV Chefs tell us to break off and throw away! I know because I spent many an evening left at the table until I chewed those tough stalks of stringy fiber. Who can forget what mothers used to try to do to spinach to make it appear pleasing, only to discover it tasted like the same old stuff that not even the propaganda from Popeye cartoons could overcome. Those were the days of meat and potatoes, but not vegetables!

Because we were made to stay at the table until our vegetables were eaten, many and various schemes were devised as to how avoid eating them. Pets proved to be unreliable because they had a tendency to carry the vegetables into the room where my parents were waiting and try to eat them there on the floor causing an unending chain of consequences that lasted sometimes for days, from my mother being extremely upset that we did not like her cooking to corporal punishment meted out by my father. The most effective means of disposing of the dreaded fare other than when we were forced to eat them came with the invention of the napkin. Barely our parents' heads were turned before the napkin was full and in the trash can. And since we were supposed to take out the garbage each night anyway, it proved to be a fairly fail safe idea until it was noticed we were doing our chores without being told and it was figured out why.

My own kids behaved very similarly, and I still wonder sometimes about vegetables. I guess it must be genetic.

THINGS CONTINUED:

REVIEWS

THE CAROLINE COMMUNITY THEATRE
March, 2015

Stories of off Broadway productions are often filled with accounts of want-to-be actors or those who have seen better days, existing in a cloud of thought that they are just on the cusp of success. The result, often, is actors destroying productions and driving away patrons. All you doubters and thespian malcontents, cast your eyes forward to center stage, inhabited by the Caroline CommunityTheatre, a troupe of players who debunk the ideas of has-been and want to-be-actors.

This troupe, to the delight of their patrons and audiences, bring life and enjoyment to the plays that land their way. Whether it be in incorporating the audience as in a *Holiday Hamicide* portrayed over the past holiday season, or such productions as *The Great American Trailer Park Musical, The Kitchen Witches,* and *Sorry, Wrong Chimney,* they bring entertainment and enjoyment to those fortunate enough to watch them. These are actors who love what they do and do what they love and are not afraid to show their pleasure.

Under the leadership of Kelly and John Snead, theater in Caroline has developed a community of actors, many going back to the first days years ago when theater was held in the Bowling Green Town Hall and was referred to as the Bowling Green Community Theater. After the Town Hall, the troupe moved to the Community Center before settling into what was once Ladysmith Elementary and most recently the Caroline Diversified Learning Center. Both Sneads find themselves doing a little of everything from audiovisual to creating stage props in addition to acting.

Kelly Snead has been acting since Kindergarten in Ladysmith Primary where she played in the play, *Annie.* A 1997 graduate of Caroline High School, Kelly attended Virginia Commonwealth

University, graduating with a Bachelors degree in business. Currently, she works at BB&T. Since her beginnings in *Annie,* Kelly has remained in theater, working in the Fredericksburg Community Theater until 2003 when she became involved in the Bowling Green Community Theater.

John Snead, a Spotsylvania native and graduate of Spotsylvania High School, helped to form a theatre company while in high school. His work in theater has been mostly behind the scenes, and has become adept at the development of plays to be used in the community theater genre.

The Caroline Community Theatre, under the auspices of the Parks and Recreation Department of Caroline County, has extended themselves beyond stage performances, inviting the children of the community to learn what it is to work in the theater. Numerous workshops and camps for children ages five to thirteen years old are held each summer. This summer coming, it is hoped they will be able to begin putting on productions as part of the theater camp experience.

The actors display their talents in a small cozy theater at one end of the school where a common thread woven among the people involved exists in the artistic passion expressed. Often this is viewed as an alternative to the business of adult life. They have the chance to touch every part of the production of a play, whether playing a part in one or directing in another or using their talents to work with the children who attend classes there. It is common for members of the troupe to perform several different jobs when putting on a production. It was stated that most actors have to make their own costumes and are often called upon to help the Sneads construct the sets.

Working towards becoming a nonprofit organization, the theater does not pay the actors. Proceeds from the sale of tickets go to pay expenses incurred such as royalties for plays put on, and the cost of catered meals for a dinner theater. To watch the actors on stage, one would think they are highly paid professionals, utilizing sparse props and a stage which is made to seem larger than life by the actors inhabiting it.

This group is full of talent that has been making contributions to the community theaters in the area for years. Jo-Elsa Jordan, a graduate of George Mason University, was been involved in theater in various roles in school. When the everyday pressures of working in marketing and event planning became a burden, she began looking for an outlet for her creative talents. The Caroline Community Theatre was fortunate to be able to provide that avenue for her. In her role as Holly in the production of Holiday Hamicide, the one criticism by critics was that her role was not big enough for her. A similar criticism was made of Ashley Taylor in the same production. Taylor, a Theater Arts student at Ferrum College, was awarded Ferrum College's *Theater Arts Achievement Award* in the spring of 2013, and has been involved in community theater since that time. Josh McCormick has played in twenty productions in the area including six in Caroline. Justin Smith, who has been playing and singing for ten years is one of the seasoned actors in this troupe.

The list goes on of talent and experience that adds up to one thing: Theater arts in Caroline County is a great commodity with assets too great to ignore.

The Caroline Community Theatre. If you have not seen it, you would not believe how good a community theater can be.

LA ROSETTA
August 2015

The Chimneys building on Caroline Street has had a new resident since December 2014, one that many have already classified as a keeper. La Rosetta International Cuisine brings to Fredericksburg a taste of international cuisine that ranges from Northern Italian to Cuban to South American; all prepared very well.

For those who come to dine at La Rosetta for the first time, be forewarned, this is not your typical restaurant. General manager Jose Gonzalez called the concept they are portraying "comfortable elegance." An accurate description, La Rosetta provides excellent food in proper portions served by a wait staff that treats customers as if they were the only ones in the restaurant.

The Gonzalez family has worked in the restaurant business since 1979 when they emigrated from El Salvador. With both parents cooking for some of the nicer hotels in Northern Virginia, it became second nature for their children to follow in their footsteps. Executive Chef Freddy Gonzalez started cooking Italian at the age of sixteen and trained under a number of chefs, learning different cuisines and achieving an expertise that has to be tasted to be believed. Along with Chef Robert Gonzalez, Freddy and Sous Chef Agueda Flores provide food that makes a visit to La Rosetta a memorable experience.

From Northern Virginia to Fredericksburg included a stop in Stafford County in 2006 with the establishment of La Rosetta in Aquia area, which was a fine dining restaurant run by the Gonzalez family prior to packing up and moving to the Burg. In addition to La Rosetta, two popular restaurants, 806 Bistro on Williams Street and Soup and Taco on Caroline fall under the Gonzalez family umbrella.

Visiting La Rosetta, my wife, Diane, and I were immediately greeted by a server and Jose Gonzalez, both of whom had warm and catching smiles. We started with salads. I had a *Spinaci E Mele* which consisted of baby spinach, caramelized pecans, red apples and gorgonzola cheese all with a balsamic vinaigrette. My wife had a grilled peach salad made up of baby spinach, grilled peaches, dates and a balsamic vinaigrette. Along with the taste, the plating of these salads was amazing.

The entrees completely destroyed my idea of what an Italian food was like. The entire menu showed various dishes to enjoy, not just pasta and marinara with an occasional meatball thrown in.   I had *Paglio E Fieno*: Homemade spinach & egg capellini with sauteed shrimp, mushrooms, capers, diced tomatoes & garlic. The shrimp were done to perfection and the capellini was very thin and flavorful giving the entire dish the essence of the pasta. Diane had *Fettuccine Verde*: Homemade spinach fettuccine with lump crabmeat, mushrooms, capers, diced tomatoes, garlic, olive oil, & fresh basil. Again the pasta was razor thin, enhancing the flavors of the other ingredients. I have seen similar dishes in other restaurants covered in a cream sauce, but Chef Freddie was not afraid use an oil sauce which laid bare the intricacies of taste of the ingredients, much to our delight. With the meal I enjoyed a glass of GioCatto pinot grigio from Slovenia that was the best I have had in years of drinking wine.   A rich citrus taste was blended with an underlying flavor of honey. This medium bodied wine provided an excellent pairing with the flavorful entrees we enjoyed.

We finished our meal by sharing a dessert that our server informed us was her favorite: *Chocolate Ecstasy*: Chocolate fudge cake with raspberry ganache & vanilla ice cream. The best way to describe this dessert was by its name, ecstasy. The ganache and the fudge cake offered two flavors melded together by the vanilla ice cream.

La Rosetta offers Fredericksburg diners a chance to taste a cuisine that is wonderfully authentic to its origins and flavorful in an atmosphere that is not pretentious, but rather comfortable. Our server, who seemed to appear at exactly the right moment to take care of our culinary needs, was very knowledgeable about the menu and answered questions we had without hesitation. Jose Gonzalez stated they were trying to provide a place where one could find great food, good service and a comfortable atmosphere. La Rosetta has achieved that and more.

SAMMY T'S
October, 2015

For the past thirty four years, storefronts and businesses have come and gone on Caroline Street in Fredericksburg, but there remains one business that has been consistent throughout that time: Sammy T's at 801 Caroline Street. This iconic Fredericksburg landmark started on Valentine's Day, 1981 and has continued to give generations of residents of the area as well as college students and visitors excellent service and food since that time.

Built in 1805, the building housing Sammy T's has included a number of different businesses including an auction house, a residence, a post office, and an auto supply store. In the 30's, a restaurant, Dugan's, opened there and remained until 1980, when it was purchased by Dr. Samuel T. Emory, a geography professor at the then Mary Washington College. Dr. Emory started Sammy T's and it has remained in the family since then. In July, 2008, Dr. Emory's wife, Sibby, died, followed by his death, in August, 2008. The Emory's son, Sam, Jr. passed away April, 2010, at which time the property was passed on to four family members, three of whom reside in Florida and one in North Carolina.

The restaurant's saving grace since then has been general manager, Jimmy Crisp, who was instructed by the family not to change a thing, but keep Sammy T's running as usual. Crisp is not your typical restaurant manager. A laid back, quiet man, it is evident he is working in something he loves. Crisp remains the general manager to this day, doing what he has done best for the past seventeen years: managing one of Fredericksburg's most beloved restaurants.

Starting out in residential construction with his brother, Crisp, who was acquainted with both Samuel and Sibby, was asked to take over managing the business. He stated it was very fast paced with quite a learning curve, and involved working a lot of nights.

"I love the people and the business. There are adults who come here who first came as children. I see some of the same tourists coming in year after year," he said.

When asked why he remained as manager for so long, Crisp remarked, "I wouldn't want to do anything else."

The major factor that has kept the doors open at Sammy T's, according to Crisp, was the restaurant has been consistent in its approach for all these years. It was noted that very little has actually changed in the operating procedures since Emory first opened the doors. In 1981, a vegan and vegetarian menu was introduced because there was no restaurant of note in the area that provided a menu similar. Crisp said that many of the original recipes are still being used and there are some employees whose years of tenure go into double digits.

The theme of consistency has paid dividends as Sammy T's has won numerous awards ranging from Best Veggie Restaurant to Best Veggie Menu. They have been named the Third Best Vegan/ Vegetarian Restaurant in the State of Virginia by Virginia Living Magazine. Most patrons, according to Crisp, come back and bring friends, delighting in a menu that meets the culinary needs of a totally diverse population.

The favorites, as seen by Crisp, are:

From The Vegetarian Menu:
Camper's Special - grilled bean & grain burger mixture wrapped in a grilled flour tortilla with sautéed onions, green peppers, tomatoes, mushrooms, Chi Chi and topped with melted mozzarella and cheddar cheese, served with a side of Lemon Tahini.

From The Vegan Menu:
Felafel- a mid-eastern dish made with chick peas, wheat germ, onion, garlic and spices - deep fried and served in a pita with

fresh mixed greens, cucumbers, red onion and our Lemon Tahini sauce.

From <u>The Standards Menu:</u>
Gourmet Hamburger - seven ounces of lean, ground, seasoned beef grilled to your specifications on a multigrain roll with lettuce, tomato and red onion, with or without cheese and/or bacon.

Now, after thirty four years, a chill has gone through the Downtown Fredericksburg community with the news that Sammy T's is up for sale. Understandably, the four family owners are finding it difficult to operate the restaurant from a long distance. Crisp commented that there are several serious buyers looking, and they all agree on one thing: Sammy T's must remain as it has been for thirty four years. Crisp stated that whatever the outcome of the sale, he hopes he can still remain as the general manager.

"This restaurant has been around for thirty four years and I hope it is around for at least thirty four more," remarked Crisp.

Crisp's remarks reflect the sentiment of all those who have supported Sammy T's since 1981. It remains a legacy not only to the Emory family, but to the historic district of downtown Fredericksburg as well.

NEWTOWN DRAGWAY

July, 2014

It is Friday night and a large number of Caroline County residents, with the majority from Sparta, are at one of the best kept secrets in the region, the Newtown Dragway. At twelve dollars a ticket, it provides a lot of good entertainment for those who come.

Two thirty five foot wide lanes extend three hundred feet with over nine hundred feet of shutdown awaits each pair of drag racers as they make it down the staging lanes from the pits, offering excitement for varying crowds of people. Because the track is made up of sand, when the race starts, the first thing one sees is sand flying everywhere. After several runs, the track is put back together by tractors that smooth out and drag the strip.

Everything from rails (super modified dragsters) to modified trucks to street trucks are ready to show what they can do. Young and old represent the surrounding counties and beyond in either Bracket Races or the *Bean Field Races,* for which the track is most noted.

"The Bean Field races started, " commented track owner and president Willard Hammond, "when farmers would cut the beans in a field. One hundred yards would be stepped off and people would come and race their trucks on the make shift drag strip."

These days the races are a considerably more organized, complete with a lighted tree to start the racers and a digital clock at the end of the track for everyone to see the times run. The times vary from the faster modified vehicles running below four seconds at speeds of ninety miles per hour or more to street vehicles running in the eight second range and above. On the nights when the Bean Field Races are held, also known as *Test*

129

and Tune, street trucks run against each other and often "grudge matches" are the order of the night in order to determine bragging rights until the next race.

On the nights when the bracket races are run, each truck is given three practice runs and the top eight times compete against each other in single elimination races until a winner is determined.

Devin Knowles, a Sparta native, stated he comes to the track every Friday night and has been racing ever since he was too young to drive on the streets, taking his Blazer to the line and running regularly between 8.20 and 8.30 seconds. Knowles commented that he does not expect to win anything, but races because it is fun to get out there and compete against other trucks.

Todd Beazley, another Spartan, commented that he raced when he was a kid and now that his children have all grown and left the house, he is racing again for the fun of it. Beazley races a street legal 2003 GMC Duramax Diesel and besides having fun, holds the diesel truck record at the track with a time of 5.371 seconds.

A lot of the participants have obviously modified vehicles with fancy paint jobs advertising their sponsors. At the Newtown Dragway, however, the fancy stuff means nothing, particularly when a rusted out bucket of bolts runs at 3.67 seconds and leaves one of the pretty cars behind eating sand.

With attendance reaching as much as twelve hundred on Bean Field Race nights, many of the spectators live vicariously through those who are racing while seated in lounge chairs either in front of or in the bed of pick up trucks enjoying their favorite beverage and commenting on their favorite drivers. A camaraderie exists among the spectators with much laughter and good times existing. Depending on whether your point of origin is King and Queen County or from as far as King George County, those people will be adamant that they are about the only ones there.

Devin Knowles' companions, Dakota Taylor and Amber Nadeau, both 2014 graduates of Caroline High School, said they come to the Newtown Dragway"...because it is fun to watch the different trucks race and is something to do on a Friday night."

The Sparta neighbors seem to find each other out, even for the most come lately to the area. Mike Shamblin and Terry Harrison know no strangers and provide quite an education to the novice sand drag fan. No one gives addresses in Sparta, it always some landmark such as "the hog field on Sparta Road," but everyone knows where it is, and after the geography is settled, the conversation goes back to racing.

Not only are the spectators known to each other, but the drivers are also known by those in attendance. Often comments concerning the driver's past genealogy or such as "The driver of that modified Isuzu is married to the driver of the rail" are heard.

When the sun starts to set and the lights come on, people are still having fun, but the races take on a serious nature as the final eight come down the staging lanes to the starting line. Spectators are riveted to the starting tree and then, as the racers go down the track and finish, the digital clock becomes the focus of attention.

It should be noted that these racers are not the loud ear splitting noise makers like the ones that run a quarter mile track and require a parachute to stop. On Saturdays, ATV's and motorcycles run. Periodically during the year, invitational events are scheduled that provide quality racing to observe. It is entertainment that people need to see to believe and understand.

For those who have not been to the Newtown Dragway, every effort needs to be made to go there at least once and experience quality family entertainment at a great price.

GOOD LUCK CELLARS
September, 2014

Katie and Paul Krop have done something that takes more than just good luck. They have taken a piece of land used as a sand and gravel pit for forty or fifty years, denuded of all top soil and then strewn with concrete rip rap and stumps and turned it into Good Luck Cellars, a beautiful vineyard and winery that is becoming a community and cultural center just outside the town of Kilmarnock.

"Restoring the grounds took two thousand bales of hay and a lot of seed," according to Krop.

After buying the property in 2004, planting began in 2005 under the watchful eye of Bill Swain, who was at the time the winemaker at Ingleside Vineyards and Winery. After the retirement and relocation of Swain, Tom Payette took over the job of consultant and remains in that position. Besides sand and gravel, there is a lot of clay in the soil, making Good Luck Cellars similar to the Bordeaux region of France.

Originally planted were thirteen acres, but with the recent addition of eight more acres planted, the vineyard has increased to twenty one acres. Krop stated they have twelve varieties of grapes, from which they are able to produce thirteen different wines. The Inheritage Vintage 2010 has the distinction of earning a Virginia Governor's Cup 2013 Bronze Medal. This is the winery's premier signature red wine blend, this wine is a full bodied and well balanced wine, made up of Cabernet Sauvignon, Cabernet Franc and Petit Verdot.

Protecting the vines are fifteen Walker hounds, brought in by Terry Dort of Select Properties, who walks and trains the dogs to stay on certain parts of the vineyard. All of the dogs are rescue dogs who become acclimated to the weather and stay outside all year. Night time finds them in insulated dog hotels where they gather several in each and provide one another comfort.

In a previous life, Paul Krop was a orthopedic surgeon who specialized in surgery on hands. Katie, an RN, was his office manager and wearer of many hats as needed in the practice. Empty nesters, the Krop decided to move to Kilmarnock from Virginia Beach to start Good Luck Cellars so they would have something to do in retirement.

"It is a seven day a week, ten to twelve hours a day job, we are always here," said Krop, "but there is something about being close to the soil, sun, rain and changing elements."

The winery building is more than just a tasting room. Entering the front door, one is struck by the pleasant, home like atmosphere in the design of the room. Directly behind the tasting room is a large room giving the idea of tabula rosa, crying out to be used in a variety of ways. Krop reported that a number of weddings and receptions are held there, with the next four weekends completely booked. Upstairs is a cupola from which can be seen the entire area, a highlight for any visitor.

The basement contains the winery, where Krop makes three to four thousand cases of wine each year. At present, ninety five percent of the barrels used for aging is French Oak. The future barrels will be American Oak, because of the flavor profile. Krop mentioned American Oak provides more of a soft, vanilla taste he is looking for in his wines. Reds wines are aged eighteen to twenty months and the whites six prior to bottling.

With a vision of not being merely a winery with a wedding venue, the Krops are expanding their use of Good Luck Cellars facilities. In addition to weddings, book signings of prominent people often take place there. A retired White House chef, who worked through five presidents recently presented a book he had written. Notables such as former governor Linwood Holton who lives in the area attended the presentation. Washington Post columnist Bob Woodward's wife had a book signing as well. Krop reported these events are always packed out.

Krop mentioned he is a board member of the Northern Neck Orchestra and hopes to have performances at the winery. The Capital Opera of Richmond will be performing selections from their 2014-2015 season at Good Luck Cellars.

For those who have watched the wine industry in Virginia, the evolution has been amazing. Now one can observe the next step of this development. Good Luck Cellars is more than an established winery with weddings on the side, it has become a cultural center in the Northern Neck.

ROGERS FORD FARM WINERY
January, 2014

Tucked away in a corner of Fauquier County, behind a small hamlet known as Summerduck, lies a true Virginia treasure. Because Summerduck is known primarily for its raceway, who would have thought a winery would fit in this locale?

The winery is located at the historic Roger's Ford, where it is said Confederate and Union troops repeatedly forded the Rappahannock River between Culpeper County and Fauquier County. On a fifty five acre tract of land located next to the C.F. Phelps Wildlife Management Area, Rogers Ford Farm Winery offers visitors a breath of fresh air away from the hectic sprawl that is becoming Route 17 outside of Fredericksburg.

In its prime the estate that the Puckett family now owns once was 1,000 acres. Seated on the estate is the farm house, circa 1825 which was the Puckett family home when they purchased the property in 1979. Johnny, son of winery founder John Puckett, lived there until recently when he moved to Fredericksburg to be closer to work. Now the house has been renovated to contain the tasting room.

Upon entering the house originally made from trees felled on the property, one is greeted by a fire place that exudes the warmth that is always found there. As striking as the fireplace is, the yellow pine flooring laid out with different widths is the first thing that catches your eye as you enter. An addition was added in 1900 and the contrast is seen between the work of the two eras of construction. The beams in the older part were notched by hand and numbered when the house was built. Many of the windows still are of the wavy design seen in older homes.

The front room has been converted into the tasting room displaying a curved bar with the tops of wine bottles that have been cut off and attached. Again the yellow pine flooring stands out and adds to the ambience of this historic place.

As lovely as this house is, it does not compare to the wines that are served. John Puckett, an aeronautical engineer, decided he wanted to start a winery and put his family to work growing an experimental crop to see what would make it. Although recently retired, allowing Johnny to take over the operation, John is still around giving sound viticultural and enological advice to any willing to receive from his rich years of experience.

On the farm, the Pucketts grow mainly Vidal Blanc and Petit Verdot, with the rest of the grapes used coming from a group of vineyard owners in central Virginia and Northern Neck. From these grapes are produced wines that reflect the current trend in Virginia wines, excellence and maturity.

Among the whites produced is an unoaked Chardonnay produced in the New Zealand style which bears the name and picture of John's oldest grandson, Jacob Christopher. This Chardonnay is very aromatic wine with just a taste of sweetness that makes it an excellent pairing with veal or seafood, or just by itself.

Another of John's grandchildren's names adorns a white blend that has been extremely popular ever since it came out. Lily Grace is a white blend of chardonnay, viognier and Vidal blanc. A light, oaked wine that is the perfect wine for shrimps on the barbie. Many drinkers of this wine prefer it as a chaser for luscious Virginia raw oysters. Another wine that is great as a solo, Lily Grace cries out for the warm summer afternoons and evenings.

Rogers Ford's best wines, many say, are their reds. In 2008, John made a bordeaux style red that is just coming into its prime. Virginia Red Select is an unfiltered blend of Cabernet Franc, Cabernet Sauvignon and Petit Verdot, this wine is a must for the red wine drinker who loves Italian meals.

In 2011, the latest vintage of Virginia Red Select to be released was made. An oaked blend of 75% Syrah, 15% Cabernet Franc and 10% Petit Verdot, this blend differs from the normal Virginia bordeaux style delivering a bold, intense structure that is an education in itself to the most informed palette. Although it is a very drinkable wine at present, it is still young and will only get better with age. Only 55 cases were produced, so it is a wine to buy now and set aside for as long as 5-10 years.

Petit Verdot is one of the five Bordeaux grapes used for mixing in France, where the growing season is much shorter. The Petit Verdot grapes never fully ripen, thus the name Petit Verdot, or little green. In Virginia, where we have a longer growing season that affords the opportunity to enjoy the full ripeness of this wonderful varietal, Rogers Ford has produced a wine that is unfiltered with a robust taste screaming for a big roast with Yorkshire pudding and all the trimmings, or at least prime rib. The Petit Verdot is bottled in a uniquely styled bottle with handles on each side of the neck ordered from the manufacturer in Italy.

Brandy Station Dulce is a Rogers Ford wine made from the Vidal Blanc grapes and then distilled into brandy and blended with more Vidal Blanc wine. Packing a punch at 18% alcohol, this sherry style wine is an aperitif that only requires a thimble full to bring a warm fuzzy feeling.

Sometimes meeting people can be an experience in itself. The Pucketts are that kind of people, warm and enjoyable. The beauty of their farm vineyard and the wonder of their wines make a trip to Sumerduck well worth it.

GARY AND LINDA: NO BARBIE AND KEN
August 2011

The thought of someone in the wedding business usually brings to mind an individual who has spent their lives fantasizing about the perfect wedding with Prince Charming on his white horse and the beautiful princess adorned just so, in a fairy tale setting. Not at Eden Try. While the region's premier wedding venue located in Spotsylvania County does offer a fairy tale setting, neither Gary Gratopp nor Linda Morrison led the charmed Barbie and Ken type of life one may think of when visiting there.

A Michigan native, Gary Gratopp has always been a business man even while attending Ferris State College where he studied business and drama. Gary reported throwing parties at his family home, charging those who attended and then splitting the proceeds with a few friends that helped in the event.

After college, at the suggestion of a friend, Gary applied with the Detroit police department where he was immediately hired. Fresh out of college with a profound street naiveté, Gary was immediately challenged when approaching a suspect, found himself flat on his back with the suspect on top soiling his brand new shiny uniform while beating him in the face. His experienced partner laughed and said, "College boy, cuff 'em first, talk to them later." Apparently Gary learned quickly, soon becoming a plain clothes officer and undercover detective in major crimes.

While working for the police department, Gary ventured into real estate, buying and renovating homes, amassing an inventory of higher end residences. After ten years in law enforcement, Gary was forced to retire due to injuries sustained on the job (it was reported he has had approximately fourteen operations) and went into the family business marketing color to show case products, a field he has expanded and is still involved in today.

Linda Morrison has led no fairy tale life. Born in October, the ninth child of single mother whose coal mining husband had abandoned the family, there was no money for any medical care so Linda was born in a convent in Hazzard, Kentucky. Sworn to a vow of poverty, the nuns had no heat, and because she weighed only two and one half pounds at birth, Linda was carried constantly and held close to absorb what body heat she could. The following Thanksgiving, she was adopted and raised by Russ and Mary Rolfes.

Refusing assistance for school from her father, a career federal government employee, Linda began working for the government after graduating from high school, and for the next fifteen years attended night school, completing her college degree in business management and contract administration. Working for the DOD, she transferred to the FAA where she recently chose an early retirement while still at the top of her profession and is now under contract to the government as a consultant.

The fairy tale begins with Gary walking his mother down the aisle to marry Linda's father. Here Gary and Linda met but did not ride off into the sunset. They remained friends for four or five years and then started a long distance relationship which has developed into what they now have. Soon after their relationship began, Linda decided to invest in some of Gary's renovation projects. The very first one she participated in was said to have brought her to tears at the idea of putting money into a house that apparently was in much need of repair. Reassured of Gary's proficiency in remodeling, she was very pleased with the outcome.

While remodeling Eden Try (which was supposed to be only an investment project), both Gary and Linda were approached by lots of people who wanted to either have their wedding pictures taken or their actual wedding to occur there. It did not take long for the marketing mind of Gary and the business management acumen of Linda to figure out what they had. From these beginnings Eden Try has grown and continues to grow and develop into the leading wedding site for the entire Fredericksburg area.

UNQUENCHABLE: A TIPSY QUEST FOR THE WORLD'S BEST BARGAIN WINES
November, 2010

Natalie MacLean's *Unquenchable: A Tipsy Quest for the World's Best Bargain Wines* is one of the books that will remain on my active bookshelf as an important piece of reference material as well as being a great read.

In her quest, Ms. MacLean finds not only bargains, but also goes into some depths as she travels to different areas around the globe where wines are made. Her style of writing gives the reader an insiders view of what goes into the production of a wine in a particular region and what makes it so unique. For example her piece about the Rieslings of Germany gives a whole new appreciation of a wine that is often in our American viewpoint considered only for women and sissies. Although I have long appreciated a good Riesling, my understanding of it was heightened by what Ms. MacLean had to say.

Natalie MacLean's humor and storytelling alone is worth the price of the book. Far from being a wine snob, she inserts in this book the pure joy of wine along with the many anecdotal comments as she continues her process of educating the reader. That being said, even if one has no interest in wine (oh, cruel throw of dice), *Unquenchable* will leave the reader with a sense of pure enjoyment at her excellent style, and if not careful, they may learn something of the various cultures and geography in this wonderful world of wine in which we live.

A very important aspect of *Unquenchable: A Tipsy Quest for the World's Best Bargain Wines* is its value as a reference. Ms. MacLean does not approach wine from the popular angles that make her love of wine and its buzz a fad. She gives the reader a truly fundamental basis for what wine is and its effect on the areas where individual varietals are produced.

Unquenchable is a must read for all who enjoy reading and an excellent reference for even the most advanced vinophile.

THE CABOOSE
July 2009

I don't know enough about Ashland to know which side of the tracks is the wrong side, but I do know on the west side lies one of the hallmarks of the business community. Although it may be easy to miss if you are not paying attention, it is worth the effort to find and stop in at The Caboose Wine Shop, just two doors down from the Iron Horse Restaurant, and peruse what Ian Kirkland and his staff have to offer.

Ian Kirkland is, in every sense of the word, a true entrepreneur. Starting out at the Iron Horse restaurant and swiftly gaining a reputation as an exceptional bar tender, Ian partnered with the owner of Iron Horse to open the Caboose in 1995 in a building that had recently been creatively renovated. At the age of twenty five, never mind the fact that he had just earned a bachelor's degree from the Savannah College of Art and Design in commercial design and the world was his oyster for the taking, Ian dove head first into this venture and his ability to focus and learn became evident quickly. Admittedly a student of craft beer as can be seen in his collection of domestic and international beer containers (a must see for all tourists and residents alike), his knowledge of wines and acute business sense is not something of which one can make light.

Even in an economy which at best is said to be somewhat shaky, Ian has worked to support a core of customers that range from Caroline County to Montpelier and as far as Richmond. His idea that "although the market is down, it must be kept interesting for the customers" comes to life with deals that he passes on from multiple vendors who are pleased to serve his establishment. Scouting the market for excellent wines, he understands that the average consumer should not have to take out a loan to get a good bottle of wine. Kirkland provides for his customers a large number of very fine and well known wines priced less than ten dollars.

The obvious camaraderie that exists there between staff and customers is very touching. One can almost see the pot bellied stove sitting in the middle of the store and people sitting around swapping yarns or the gossip of the day. One such customer, Bud Watson (a regular), said the reason he comes in (besides the fact that staff member Shannon Cooke is there) is because the store is such a nice place to visit. Added reasons Mr. Watson stated were the weekly wine tastings and "First Friday Beer Tastings."

I must agree that Shannon is an excellent reason to visit the Caboose not only because of her excellent customer service but also because of the wonderful job she does making sure there are up to date and first-rate cheeses and appetizers available for every taste in wine or beer. As I was leaving she handed me a small pepper stuffed with a cream cheese mixture that made me think about camping out and just staying there.

It's no small wonder Bud Watson is a regular, I do not plan on being a stranger.